Langston Hughes in Lawrence

Photographs and Biographical Resources

by

Denise Low & T. F. Pecore Weso

Photographs by Denise Low

MAMMOTH PUBLICATIONS
Lawrence, Kansas 66044-4540

Book design by Paul Hotvedt
Blue Heron Typesetters
729½ Massachusetts St.
Lawrence, KS 66044

Mammoth Publications
1916 Stratford Rd.
Lawrence, KS 66044-4540
mammothpubs@hotmail.com

ISBN: 0-9761773-3-1

Cover portrait by Winold Reiss (1886-1953). The artist's son
donated Reiss's pastel drawing of poet Langston Hughes to
the National Portrait Gallery in his father's memory.

Printed on acid-free paper.

Photograph of boys fishing is in the Watkins Community
Museum collection, courtesy of Ed Bumgardner.

To Sonny Kenner

Kansas City musician
(1933–2001)

Our Muse

who taught us how to listen
to music of the past

and how to stay
on the sunny side of the street

Contents

Introduction

The first place I remember is Lawrence, right here. And the specific street I remember is Alabama Street. And then we moved north, we moved to New York Street, shortly thereafter. The first church I remember is the A.M.E Church on the corner of Ninth, I guess it is, and New York. That is where I went to Sunday School, where I almost became converted, which I tell about in The Big Sea.

Langston Hughes, public lecture "Life Makes Poetry," at
the University of Kansas, 28 April 1965.[i]

In 2004, the Academy of American Poets named Langston Hughes's boyhood home in Lawrence, Kansas, a national poetry landmark. Lawrence residents have been aware of his imprint on the town, especially since the 1970s when Katie Armitage, Elizabeth Schultz, Paulette Sutton, William Tuttle, and others began to reconstruct Hughes's boyhood years in Lawrence, from about 1903 to 1915. Almost from his birth in 1902, city documents show Lawrence was home base to the boy Langston. His mother appears in the city directory of 1903, and her minor child would be with her, though unlisted. Langston Hughes himself appears on the 1905 Kansas census, with his grandmother and not his mother. In his autobiography, he reports he lived with his mother in Topeka in 1908, but he omits the early Lawrence years.[ii] Because his maternal grandmother Mary Langston lived in Lawrence, Hughes had a connection to the town beginning from his birth in nearby Joplin, Missouri. Some scholars, like Maria Butler, date his Lawrence years as 1902–1915.

Many sites where Hughes lived, worked, played, and studied are still accessible. Oak Hill Cemetery holds graves of his grandparents, two uncles, and at least one cousin. Because Lawrence has many buildings on historic registers, which prohibits their demolition, a surprising number of them remain intact.

i Quoted in "Exhibit Honors Poet Who Drew from Life in Lawrence," *Lawrence Journal World* 15 Feb. 1981.

ii Katie Armitage, video lecture, Academic Outreach Program, *Biography of a City: Lawrence* (Session 7B), 1998. Hughes appears in his grandmother's household, without his mother Carrie Langston Hughes.

A local business occupies his grandfather's downtown grocery building. Central School, where Hughes attended junior high, now serves as an office complex. The streets of today's Lawrence still have recognizable sights from Hughes's and his mother's times, such as the courthouse, Kansas Seed Company, Union Pacific depot, post office (Seventh and New Hampshire Sts.), and Bowersock Opera House. Two churches Hughes's family attended, St. Luke AME and Warren (Ninth) St. Baptist Church, retain their original buildings, and both have active congregations.

This book assembles photographs of sites and buildings referred to by Hughes in his autobiography *The Big Sea,* in the autobiographical novel *Not Without Laughter,* and places referenced by biographers. Where buildings have been torn down, vintage photographs show original structures.

Sections include clustered sites: downtown Lawrence; Central Lawrence and the Pinckney neighborhood, just west of downtown; the University of Kansas; East Lawrence and New York St.; Oak Hill Cemetery; Woodland Park; and the outlying area of Lakeview. The downtown and East Lawrence sites are within easy walking distance. The other areas are accessible by car.

Downtown begins with the visitors' center at the Union Pacific depot of North Lawrence, just northeast of the Kaw River Bridge and City Hall. The route continues south on Massachusetts St., which was named after the abolitionist state responsible for founding Lawrence. All of downtown Lawrence is on the state historic register. William Quantrill and his men destroyed most buildings from the earliest years in the raid of 1863. The efforts of the Lawrence Preservation Alliance and other individuals and organizations have preserved many late 19th and early 20th Century buildings. Brass markers on each downtown building give information about date of construction, architectural style, and history.

The **Central** area just west of Downtown includes the Alabama St. home site of Hughes's grandmother; the next-door house where his uncle lived; and a 19th century house identical to the grandmother's house; the **Pinckney Neighborhood,** including his teacher's house; and, on Ninth St., original buildings of the Baptist church, Central School, and the former Lawrence Public Library.

Both Hughes and his mother were familiar with the **University of Kansas**. It has few buildings from the time when Hughes's mother attended classes 1894 to 1895; and the anatomy building where Hughes says he watched dissections is gone. A new football stadium covers the former field where he watched games against Missouri and Nebraska, about four blocks from his grandmother's house. However, the student union, where Hughes presented readings as an adult, remains. Also, the Spencer Research Library has a collection of 300 items, many of them donated by the author and autographed.

The **East Lawrence** of Langston Hughes includes the Santa Fe Railroad (Seventh St. and New Jersey St.); New York St. and the St. Luke AME church building (900 New York St.); Hughes's fourth through sixth grade school site; and the home site of James and "Auntie" Mary Reed (731 New York St.). An old stone barn in the alley of New York St. dates from Hughes's time.

Beyond the immediate center of Lawrence are several sites important to Langston Hughes.

Oak Hill Cemetery, in Far East Lawrence, includes graves of Charles and Mary Langston; their two sons Desalines[iii] and Nathaniel; Rev. Mercer, former pastor of Ninth St. Baptist Church; Henry Copeland, brother to one of John Brown's Harper's Ferry group; and former slaves. Victims of Quantrill's raid are buried here, along with other anti-slavery citizens James H. Lane, John Speer, and Dr. Charles L. Robinson. George Nash Walker, famous Vaudeville entertainer, is also buried here.

Woodland Park, now overgrown, is just west of the cemetery. It was the setting of a scene in *Not Without Laughter*, where African American children were excluded from a city celebration. Brook Creek Park playground is here, but all that remains of the large amusement park are a few concrete foundations and hiking trails through the woods. The trailhead is near the intersection of Twelfth St. and Prairie Ave.

Lakeview, where the Langston grandparents resided from 1870 until 1886, is about five miles northwest of Lawrence on the river road winding west toward Lecompton. Now the oxbow lake is a private club, but the fields around the lake show the richness of this bottomlands area. About two hundred species of birds, including many waterfowl, live in this area. A visit to Lakeview shows the agricultural roots of Langston Hughes's family.

Of course, the climate and geography are the same through the hundred years since Langston Hughes lived here. Large yards of central Lawrence still teem

[iii] We found this son's name spelled "Dessalines" (after the Haitian revolutionary Jean Jacques Dessalines), "Desalines," and "Desaline." His marriage license uses the spelling "Desaline." The city directory lists him as "D. W. Langston." He may have been Charles H. Langston's son from a wife previous to Mary Sampson Patterson Langston. He appears to have dropped the "Jean Jacques" and added the "W.," perhaps a reference to his mother's family.

with wildlife (foxes, opossums, squirrels, rabbits, raccoons, garter snakes); gardens and grape arbors are still common; and the Kaw (Kansas) River is a constant presence. When he lived in Harlem, Hughes cultivated a small garden outside his stoop, hardly a square yard in size.[iv] Perhaps this plot recalled childhood years of planting and harvesting subsistence foods in Kansas soil.

Hughes was a remarkable talent. Whether his own nature resulted in genius or whether nurturance in the Lawrence area abetted this talent is an irresolvable question. Nonetheless, some of the same influences, in flora as well as architecture and social milieu, persist at this crossroads town. His grandparents' personal cause of abolitionism is still celebrated in local histories. At the same time, racial inequities continue to exist. In his writings Hughes recalls the difficult times he had in Lawrence, as well as the better times. No sorrow was absolute; no joy was unmitigated. The paradoxes of a border state remain to this day. Nonetheless, in the year 2000, *U.S.A. Today* ranked Lawrence as one of the least segregated communities in the U.S.

This book is made possible by the wonderful scholarship already completed about the life of Langston Hughes in Lawrence, both nationally and locally. Spencer Library began a collection of the author's works during the 1950s. Katie Armitage first assembled information about buildings from Langston Hughes's time and made these available to Arnold Rampersad and the community. In the 1970s, Lawrence school children celebrated Langston Hughes during National Children's Book Week. This included a talk by John Taylor, Hughes's former school friend, and Miss Ida Lyons, his former teacher. Members of the local 1976 bicentennial commission funded a statue of Hughes for the local history museum. Scholars collected oral interviews with remaining friends and family members. In 1980 the city commemorated Hughes with a quotation on the new city hall, "We have tomorrow/ Bright before us/ Like a flame." The Lawrence Arts Center and Raven Bookstore have sponsored a writing contest in Hughes's name since 1995.

The 21st century in Lawrence opened with the 100-year anniversary of Hughes's birth celebrated by a nationally televised symposium. Alice Walker, Amira Baraka, Arnold Rampersad, Danny Glover, and many others contributed to the event, co-chaired by Maryemma Graham and William Tuttle of the Uni-

---

[iv] James Haskins, *The Life of Langston Hughes* (Trenton: Africa World Press, 1993), 140.

versity of Kansas.[v] Following this was the K.U. Langston Hughes National Poetry Project, "Speaking of Rivers: Taking Poetry to the People." The Lawrence Preservation Alliance continues to advocate for the historic integrity of the town.

All of these good works, and those that will continue in the future, inspire this book. The great writer himself inspires this book.

A special thank you to Jaclyne A. Houe, clerk in the Douglas County Register of Deeds Office, who led us through the maze of files. Appreciation goes to Paul Hotvedt, our designer and supporter, who barters for the right goods. Members of La Prima Tazza group—especially Donald Knight, Gary Marshall, and Keith Fellenstein—were helpful in readjusting our view of Lawrence to early 20th century sights. Our appreciation to Keith Fellenstein for the photograph of Woodland Park coins. Daniel Low contributed to our project with wise suggestions. Caryn Goldberg helped with reading earlier versions and friendship. The Imagination & Place group inspired us to look at the beautiful world beneath our feet.

The staff of the Lawrence Public Library also helped immeasurably, living up to a legacy that stretches back to Langston Hughes himself. Our best wishes to all.

Many people assisted with this venture, and we acknowledge them, but all errors are our own.

Denise Low and T.F. Pecore Weso
Lawrence, 2004

[v] Also involved with the symposium were John Edgar Tidwell, Elizabeth Schultz, Carmaletta Williams, Barbara Watkins, Sandra Weichart, Chancellor Robert E. Hemenway, and others. C-SPAN recorded many of the events.

DOWNTOWN LAWRENCE

↑ North

KANSAS RIVER

Union Pacific RR
402 N. 2nd St.

City Hall 6 E. 6th St

6th St.

Law. Natl Bank
700 Mass. ■

■ **Bowersock** 642 Mass.

7th St.   **Eldridge** ■
701 Mass.

8th St.

■ **Barteldes** 804 Mass.

■ **Grocery** 820 Mass.

Warehouse ■
803 N.H.

■ **Patee Th. Site** 828 Mass.

9th St.

10th St.

Watkins 1047 Mass. ■

11th St.

■ **Dg. Co.**
Courthouse 1100 Mass.

12th St.

Vermont St.

Mass. St.

New Hamp.St.

*Union Pacific Railroad Depot, now the Lawrence Information Visitor Center, 402 N. Second St. (two blocks north of the Massachusetts St. bridge over the Kansas River) (1889)

This depot, built in 1889, was the place where soldiers departed during World War I and World War II. Langston Hughes and his family would have seen this building in their daily lives and may have used this depot for trips to Topeka and Kansas City. Freight trains still roll through the station but do not stop here.

Today the restored building serves the Lawrence area as an information center, where historic pamphlets and walking tour information are available. When the Union Pacific closed the station in 1984, the company planned to demolish it. Community donations and grants were used to renovate the building. It re-opened in 1996.

* Denotes an original 19th or early 20th century building throughout this book.

Union Pacific Railroad Depot, 402 N. Second St. (two blocks north of the Massachusetts St. bridge over the Kansas River)

This vintage photograph taken by E.S. Tucker shows the North Lawrence depot about 1895. Passenger service here and at the Santa Fe Depot linked Lawrence to Denver, Kansas City, and beyond.

The train ran to Denver and points further west. The railroad had a ticket office in the Eldridge House, in the 700 block of Massachusetts St.

The Union Pacific was first known as the Kansas Pacific and was Lawrence's first railroad, dating from 1864 (Tucker). One of the first branches went to the city of Leavenworth, about forty miles northeast, where Hughes's grandfather Charles Langston lived from 1863 to 1868.

Kansas River scene of boys fishing, early 20th century

This photograph shows boys sitting on the north side of the Kansas River dam looking toward Massachusetts Street, the main street of downtown Lawrence. Industrial buildings across the river, including the barbed wire factory beyond the dam, employed many workers in early Lawrence. Langston Hughes's uncle Nathaniel Turner worked in a mill near here at the time of his death in 1897. He may have died in an accident at the mill.

Langston Hughes would have seen groups like this as a boy. Fishing from the dam area of the river continues to be a popular pastime. River catfish reach up to fifty pounds at this spot on the river.

The photograph is in the Watkins Community Museum collection, courtesy of Ed Bumgardner.

Kansas River from City Hall fourth floor

The city hall has a public observation deck on its fourth floor. It overlooks the river that Hughes refers to in his autobiography. The barbed wire factory is in the right foreground, and the electricity generator building is in the middle foreground.

In the poem "The Negro Speaks of Rivers," Hughes writes,

I have known rivers:
Ancient, dusky rivers.
My soul has grown deep
   like the rivers.

When Alice Walker stayed in a hotel overlooking the river during the Langston Hughes symposium (2002), she told a University of Kansas audience that the Kaw reminded her of Hughes's years living alongside this river.

Kinetic sculpture, "Flame," City Hall, 6 East Sixth St.

The sculpture, at the southwest corner of city hall, is a companion piece to Langston Hughes's quotation inscribed on the brick wall. The sculpture, "Flame," was installed June 30, 1992.

Lin Emery, a Louisiana sculptor born in 1928, created the artwork. In an artist's statement (AskArt) she writes:

> For more than 30 years, all my sculpture has been kinetic—mainly large-scale work for public spaces. Both the forms and the random movement are inspired by nature. The linked elements may evoke plant or flying forms, and are set in motion by natural forces—wind or water. Their highly polished surfaces mirror the world around them, while their movement is influenced by infinite variables: the points of balance, the normal frequency of each element, the interruption of the counterpoise.

**Lawrence City Hall, 6 East Sixth St., intersection,
Massachusetts and Sixth**

A plaque next to the entrance of the city hall has this quote from Langston
Hughes's poem "Youth":

We have tomorrow
Bright before us
Like a flame.

In 1978 the city had a contest among school children to select a motto or quotation for the new city building. This selection by Srija Srinivasan, who was ten
at the time, won the contest. It refers to the city seal, which has a phoenix ris-
ing from ashes. In the early years of the city, fire destroyed the town twice.

***Bowersock Opera House, now known as Liberty Hall,
642 Massachusetts St. (1912)**

Langston Hughes attended theatrical events here as a boy. Among the shows he saw were *The Pink Lady* and *The Firefly*. He saw performers like dancer Ruth St. Denis, and Sothern and Marlowe. Though African Americans were allowed to attend events, they were required to sit in the balcony.

The left side of the building was the electric streetcar station that operated when Hughes was a boy and later, through the 1970s, a bus station.

Now known as Liberty Hall, the building was erected in 1912. It is in the *beaux arts* style with details of leaded glass and Doric columns. The building was one of the first downtown Lawrence buildings to be renovated in the mid-1980s.

***Bowersock Opera House, now known as Liberty Hall,
642 Massachusetts St. (1912)**

This plaque on the corner of Seventh St. and Massachusetts St. recapitulates the history of this site. *The Herald of Freedom*, funded by the Massachusetts Emigrant Aid Co., was published from 1854 to 1859. The office at this site was destroyed in Sheriff Jones's sack of Lawrence in 1856.

Liberty Hall Opera House, the next building, welcomed Oscar Wilde and other 19th century notables. After a fire destroyed the original building in 1911, J.D. Bowersock built this structure for theatrical and musical entertainment. It is still in use for both live acts and films.

The Eldridge Hotel, 701 Massachusetts St. (1926)

This is the fourth hotel on this site. Langston Hughes may have worked in the third building, around 1913. Anti-Free State raiders from Missouri burned the first two structures.

In *The Big Sea,* Hughes wrote about working in a Lawrence hotel: "When I was in the seventh grade, I got my first regular job, cleaning up the lobby and toilets of an old hotel near the school I attended. I kept the mirrors and spittoons shined and the halls scrubbed. I was paid fifty cents a week" (22).

The Eldridge Hotel displays models of the four hotels and related historic photographs. The hotel exhibits the models in different locations, depending on the season. The third model shows the hotel as it appeared from the late 1860s to 1926, when Hughes lived in Lawrence.

Free-State Hotel, 701 Massachusetts St., on the site of the present Eldridge Hotel (1913)

This is a vintage photograph of the hotel where Langston Hughes could have worked as a boy. It was built after the 1863 raid by William Quantrill. This hotel was torn down and replaced by the building that now houses the Eldridge Hotel.

In his autobiographical novel, Hughes describes brass spittoons of the hotel, and "At the rear of the lobby was the clerk's desk, a case of cigars and cigarettes, a cooler for water, and the door to the men's room" (*Not Without Laughter* 209). Another contemporaneous photograph shows a cigar counter at the back of this hotel's lobby. A women's room is now at the back of the lobby.

The photograph was taken by Alfred Lawrence around 1895.

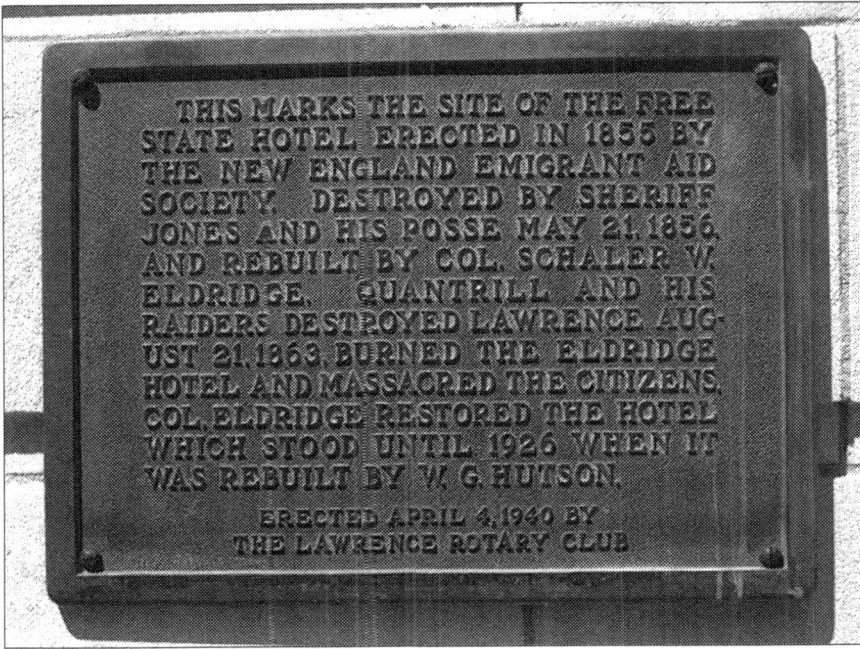

Eldridge Hotel, detail

This 1940 plaque next to the Eldridge Hotel entrance reads:

This marks the site of the free state hotel erected in 1855 by the New England Emigrant Aid Society. Destroyed by Sheriff Jones and his posse May 21, 1856, and rebuilt by Col. Schaler W. Eldridge. Quantrill and his raiders destroyed Lawrence August 21, 1863, burned the Eldridge Hotel and massacred the citizens. Col. Eldridge restored the hotel which stood until 1926 when it was rebuilt by W.G. Hutson.

Sheriff Jones and William Quantrill were pro-slavery leaders based in Missouri. The Border Wars are considered by some historians to predate the April 12, 1861, outbreak of the Civil War at Ft. Sumter, South Carolina.

Lawrence House, 811 Vermont St., demolished

This African American hotel may have been the hotel where Langston Hughes worked after school. However, in his fictionalized autobiography, his hero writes about hotel patrons who were White salesmen. In some ways, however, this structure fits Hughes's writing. He describes the "Drummer's Hotel" as: "A three-story frame structure" (*Not Without Laughter* 209).

Other hotels from that time were the Fairfax Hotel (708 Massachusetts St.), Santa Fe Hotel (700 Connecticut St.), Place House (846 New Hampshire St.), and Savoy Hotel (846 Vermont St.) (See Appendix 1). The Santa Fe was also a wooden frame building of three stories. Vermont St. was the location of African American businesses at that time. This 1895 photograph is by E.S. Tucker.

Lawrence National Bank, Seventh St. and Massachusetts St., demolished

This photograph by E.S. Tucker shows Lawrence National Bank in about 1895. The bank once stood at Seventh. St. and Massachusetts. The bank building was also the meeting place for commerce clubs. The first town library was housed in this building.

A contract signed by Langston Hughes's grandmother, Mary S. Langston, mortgaged the Langston property of 726 Alabama St. (Block 12, south half of Lot 7) to the Lawrence National Bank (see Appendix 2). The mortgage is dated 28 Feb. 1895. Alfred Whitman notarized it, and James Brooks was the register of deeds.

A.N. Fuller was the bank representative on the mortgage, even though city directories do not identify him as a banker. The 1893-94 and 1896 city directories list A.N. Fuller as a resident. In 1893-94, he is listed as a "dealer in minerals," residing on Henry St. He does not appear in the 1898 directory. In 1905, an Arthur N. Fuller resided between Winthrop and Warren Streets, with no occupation listed.

*Barteldes Seed Store, 804 Massachusetts St. (1865)

The building with the "Sunflower" sign is 804 Massachusetts. Langston Hughes writes about a boyhood job: "In the springtime I used to collect maple seeds and sell them to the seed store" (*Big Sea* 21).

In this brick building, F. Barteldes, F.W. Barteldes and M. Wilhelmi conducted a mail-order seed business. The plaque reads:

> *One of the first sites rebuilt after Quantrill's Raid in 1863. Interior destroyed by fire 1997. Restored 1997–98. Though modified several times, the Italianate store front retains many original features.*

The business began in 1860 and continued a hundred years. The company also grew seeds in nearby fields. The firm of about 35 employees had a branch in Denver. They sent out catalogues and sold seeds throughout the United States and Europe (Tucker 164). This was their retail outlet.

*Kansas (Barteldes) Seed Warehouse, 803 New Hampshire St. (1864–1890s)

Langston Hughes probably took his seeds to this warehouse rather than the retail store at 804 Massachusetts St.

The three-story building, 120 feet by 120 feet, was renovated and now includes office and retail space. The plaque at the entrance reads:

> *Typical utilitarian stone warehouse constructed between 1864–1890s in three stages. Barteldes Seed Company, founded ca. 1860, cleaned, stored, packaged, and shipped its internationally marketed products from this location until 1962.*

The founder, F. Barteldes, died in 1887, but his heirs kept the company going.

Another seed store during the time of Hughes was the W.J. Busch Seed Co. at 608 Massachusetts. It also could be the seed company Hughes knew.

*820 Massachusetts St., site of the Charles Langston and Richard Burns grocery store, 1888–92 (1866)

The awning of 820 Massachusetts now reads "Black-Eyed Susan's." The city directory listed this business as a grocery, owned by Burns and Co., with Langston Hughes's grandfather as a business associate.

According to the *Lawrence Weekly Record* obituary of 1892, Charles Langston, grandfather of Langston Hughes, moved into Lawrence in 1886 from a farm in nearby Lakeview so he could participate more fully in community life. He was, briefly, associate editor of *The Historic Times,* a local African American newspaper. He served as president of Lawrence's Colored Benevolent Society, Grand Master of the Masonic Fraternity (colored) of Kansas, and the "Counselor of the Knights of the Wise Men of the World." Langston continued to farm (he owned 26 acres at Lakeview in the 1893-94 city directory) as well as maintain his part of the grocery business until his death in 1892, at the age of 75.

In 1893-94, Nathaniel Turner Langston, Charles and Mary's son, was listed in the city directory as a grocer with Burns and Co.

**Arcade at 828 Massachusetts St., former site of the
Patee movie theater.**

In Langston Hughes's book *The Big Sea,* he recalls attending movies at the Patee movie house for five cents, until Mrs. Vivian Patee put up a sign refusing entrance to African Americans.

The theater burned down in 1955. Soon after, Penney's built the large building at 830 Mass., now the Antique Mall, and Ernst Hardware, pictured above at 826 Mass., is the other wall of the arcade. At present this is a walkway to a city parking lot.

The mural "Celebration of Cultures" was a group project created in 1995. Community members assisted Lawrence artist David Loewenstein, the designer. In 1996 Loewenstein also created a mural project for Cordley School, in honor of Hughes.

Patee Theater, 828 Massachusetts St., about 1913.

This vintage photo from a 1913 memorial album shows the Patee Theater, soon after it opened (*Lawrence Daily Journal World*).

Vivian and her husband Clair Patee were press representatives for national touring performers. At the advent of moving pictures, the Patees started the first movie theater in New Jersey.

Mrs. Patee returned to Lawrence, where she had lived as a child, to care for her stepfather, H.A. Allen. While here, she built this theater. She was born Elizabeth McFarland, and her tombstone in Oak Hill Cemetery includes the portrait that was once on the front of the theatre.

Other movie theatres in Lawrence when Hughes was a boy were, according to the 1913-1914 city directory, Airdome (834 New Hampshire St.), Bowersock (648 Massachusetts St.), Grand (736 Massachusetts St.), Nickle (708 Massachusetts St.), Oread (907 Massachusetts St.) and Palace (633 Massachusetts St.).

*Watkins Community Museum of History, formerly Watkins Bank, 1047 Massachusetts St. (1888)

Langston Hughes writes about the constant threat of foreclosure his grand-mother endured: "But we were never quite sure the white mortgage man was not going to take the house" (*Big Sea* 16).

Mark Scott suggests the "mortgage man" could be Albert L. Stanton, listed in the 1907 city directory as an employee of the Watkins Land Mortgage Co. In Hughes's autobiographical novel *Not Without Laughter*, he names the small Kansas town Stanton. However, A.N. Fuller signed the mortgage, on behalf of the Lawrence National Bank, not Stanton.

This bank is similar to the Lawrence National Bank building that no longer exists. J.B. Watkins built this red-brick structure in 1888. At one time it was the city hall. The Romanesque Revival building remains an example of opulent ar-chitectural details, especially the interior of marble and polished hardwood. Ac-cording to town lore, J.B. Watkins inspected all materials for the building and returned all that did not meet his standards.

*Watkins Community Museum of History, formerly Watkins Bank, 1047 Massachusetts St., second floor (1888)

James Patti created this life-size sculpture of Langston Hughes as a paperboy. In *The Big Sea,* Hughes remembers delivering the *Saturday Evening Post,* daily newspapers, and the *Appeal to Reason* (21-2). John Taylor, a boyhood friend of Hughes, helped Patti with details of dress.

Taylor maintained a life-long friendship and correspondence with the great writer. In 1974 he told a news reporter that Hughes sent him a copy of each new book. He remembered Hughes "was beyond most children in school and didn't need to study much." He also remembered Hughes had a sunny disposition most of the time: "He loved people, lots of people and had a ready smile. He frowned very little, but when he did, had a reason. His theory was that it took more muscles to frown than to smile." In this depiction, the young poet does smile, but also he seems reflective as well.

*Douglas County Court House, 1100 Massachusetts St. (1904)

Langston Hughes's mother Carrie Langston Hughes worked for Douglas County as a Deputy District Court Clerk in 1896, after she graduated from Emporia Normal School. Her employer was African American Sherman Harvey, the County Clerk.

This building, built in 1904, houses Douglas County offices. Langston Hughes would have known this courthouse building.

John G. Haskell, brother of the senator Dudley, designed the building with Frederick C. Gunn. The building is Romanesque Revival architectural style. Native limestone blocks are the main building material. It typifies Haskell's style as seen in several buildings throughout town.

CENTRAL LAWRENCE AND PINCKNEY

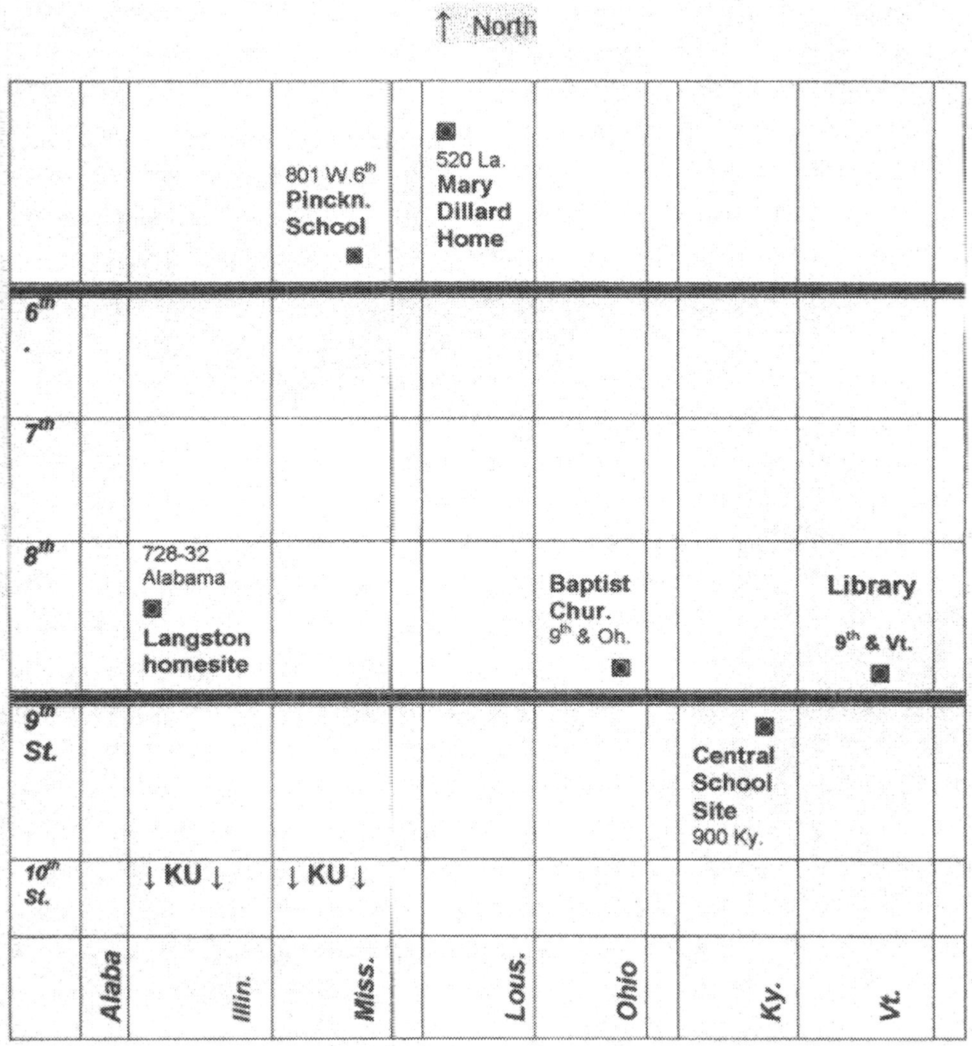

↑ North

801 W.6th
Pinckn.
School

520 La.
Mary
Dillard
Home

6th

7th

8th

728-32
Alabama
Langston
homesite

Baptist
Chur.
9th & Oh.

Library
9th & Vt.

9th
St.

Central
School
Site
900 Ky.

10th
St.

↓ KU ↓   ↓ KU ↓

Alaba   Illin.   Miss.   Lous.   Ohio   Ky.   Vt.

Homesite of Mary and Charles Langston, 1886 to 1915, 732 Alabama St.

Langston Hughes's maternal grandparents owned the house that was once on this site. Hughes remembered his grandmother telling him "long, beautiful stories about people who wanted to make the Negroes free" (*Big Sea* 17) as he grew up here.

They moved from a farm near Lakeview when Charles Langston entered the grocery business. Charles is listed in the city directory at this address in 1886. After he died (1892), Mary continued to reside here, except for when she rented it out and boarded with the Reeds on New York St. and the times she lived with her daughter Carrie and Carrie's husband, James N. Hughes, in Joplin or Mexico.

Hughes and his mother lived here intermittently throughout Hughes's childhood. The 1902-03 city directory records both Carrie M. Hughes and Mary Langston at this residence, but minor children were not listed, so Hughes was also here. The 1905 census shows the boy Hughes, age 4, living here with his grandmother Mary Langston, age 69. In the 1907 city directory, James N. Hughes, Langston's father, is listed at this residence, and his occupation is "stenographer." And in 1915, Homer Clark, Langston's stepfather, and Carrie (Langston) Clark are listed as living here.

Legal description of this property is lot 9 and the south half of lot 8, block 12 of the Lane Place subdivision. A duplex is now on this site.

**Home of Desalines W. Langston, uncle of Langston Hughes,
726 Alabama St. (1886?)**

In 1886, D.W. Langston (Desalines) lived here, according to the city directory. He was Carrie Langston's foster- or half-brother, and Langston Hughes's uncle. He also was listed as a barber on Henry St., west of Massachusetts St. The stone foundation may be original.

In 1895, Mary S. Langston, with Sarah S. Langston, mortgaged this property to A.N. Fuller of Lawrence National Bank for $125 (See Appendix 2). Legal description is "The south half of Lot number seven (7) Block twelve (12) Lane Place in the City of Lawrence." In 1909, Mary Langston and Carrie Langston Hughes sold the north half of lot 8, also described in the registry of deeds as 726 Alabama, for $175.

Hughes refers to the bank's mortgage man, who was a constant worry as the family struggled to meet payments. This house, part of the family holdings, was mortgaged to the bank.

Legal owners listed by the Douglas Co. registrar of deeds were, beginning in 1887: Mrs. S.A. Northway, J.S. Emery, Mrs. John L. Kilworth, John W. Clark, and Joseph E. Hughes. Joseph E. Hughes and then his wife Lethna retained control of the property until 1972. John W. Clark was an African American lawyer in Lawrence. Though the Langstons had title during the late 19th century, the registry of deeds does not reflect their ownership.

726 Alabama St., outbuilding in back yard (1886?)

This building is currently being used as a garage, but the door and the window in the side indicate it once was used as a home. This could have been a rental unit during the time the Langston family owned it. The 1908-1909 city directory lists Lewis Overstreet and Robert Thomas as both living at this address. This building would have been available for a second person to rent.

Hughes wrote of how his grandmother rented rooms to University of Kansas students to support the family:

> But she tried to make a living by renting rooms to college students from Kansas University; or by renting out half her house to a family; or sometimes she would move out entirely and go to live with a friend, while she rented the whole little house for ten or twelve dollars a month, to make payments on the mortgage. (Big Sea 16)

***736 Alabama St., identical to Langston house, and Ian Hurst**

Ian Hurst, owner, is restoring this late 19th century house to the original condition, as much as possible (2004 interview). According to scholar Katie Armitage, this house, next door to 732 Alabama St., is identical to the one Langston Hughes lived in with his grandmother. The house at 726 Alabama has a similar limestone foundation.

Architectural details are consistent with the date of 1886, when Hughes's grandfather and family moved from the farm in Lakeview, five miles northwest of Lawrence. Hurst dates the house to late 19th century from details of the soft bricks, window arches, and masonry. The limestone foundation is still sound, though the bricks are fragile and have deteriorated in places. This small house is six-hundred square feet in size. After completing the restoration, Hurst plans to paint the brickwork for preservation.

Deeds for this block of Lane Place Addition do not show clear property ownership before 1920 (Appendix 2). This property could have been part of the 19th century Langston holdings, especially since the city directory shows no residence at this address until 1907, when J.A. Porter is a resident.

Hurst understands from neighbors that this block had several identical houses for working class African Americans.

Pinckney School, 801 West Sixth St. (Intersection of Mississippi St. and Sixth St.) (1931)

This school site is where Langston Hughes attended elementary school from 1909 to 1910. The location is a few blocks from his grandmother's house at 732 Alabama St. Today's Pinckney School was built in 1931.

The first Pinckney School was on the front grounds of the present site. Hughes would have attended school in that building. Sixth St. was formerly known as Pinckney St.

When he was living near here, he writes of his education from his grandmother Mary Langston, who told him stories where "always life moved, moved heroically toward an end" (*Big Sea* 17).

Pinckney School entrance, 810 West Sixth St. (1931)

Pinckney students placed markers at the home sites where Langston Hughes lived and gravestones for his grandparents (donated by Rumsey Funeral Home, also on Sixth St.). According to the school website, a celebration in 1991 included dedication of a Langston Hughes Library for Children at Pinckney, and Hughes's biographer, Arnold Rampersad, attended.

Mary J. Dillard was Hughes's teacher. At that time Lawrence schools were segregated up to grade four, although the neighborhood was not segregated.

Pinckney School, 801 West Sixth St (1872)

E.S. Tucker took this photography of the old Pinckney School building in about 1895. It stood in the front yard of the present building. This school was built in 1872. In 1908 four rooms were added, so Langston Hughes attended school in a larger building. During Hughes's time there was no electricity.

Hughes began second grade here in 1909 and completed third grade before transferring to integrated New York School for the rest of the elementary grades. At Pinckney, African American students had a separate classroom and teacher, Mary Dillard. She must have made an impression on the young Hughes, as he maintained contact with her as an adult.

*Home of Mary Dillard, 520 Louisiana St. (1890s?)

When Langston Hughes attended Pinckney School, Mary J. Dillard was his teacher. This is her residence, a few blocks east of the school.

When Hughes returned to Lawrence for public readings in later years (1958, 1965), he probably stayed at her house (Armitage). The two maintained ties after he left Lawrence, including published correspondence. Area newspapers record Hughes's visits to friends and relatives in Lawrence throughout the rest of his life (see Appendix 3).

After teaching at Pinckney School, Dillard went on to become principal of Lincoln School.

*Warren St. Baptist Church, now known as Ninth St. Baptist Church, 847 Ohio St., intersection of Ninth St. and Ohio (1872)

The inset arch above the stained glass window gives the date of this building as 1872.

Warren Street Baptist Church is where Langston Hughes's grandparents and mother participated in some community services and cultural events, though they were not members. Now known as Ninth Street Baptist Church, the church continues to have an active congregation of about 250 people.

According to the Pluralism Project, the church originated in 1855 as the Second Missionary Baptist Mission in Lawrence. First services were held in a hardware store, until a wooden building was erected on this site in 1868, soon replaced by this limestone building. The church is affiliated with the National Baptist Convention.

*847 Ohio, front entrance of Ninth Street Baptist Church (1872)

When Langston Hughes had reason to enter this church, near his grandmother's house on Alabama St., it was known as the Warren Street Baptist Church. In 1945 the city changed all east-west street names to numbers. Hughes attended the funeral of vaudeville personality George (Nash) Walker here in 1911.

The building is made of hewn vernacular limestone blocks, a common building material used in the Lawrence area. According to Dr. George Wiley of the Pluralism Project, "The Ninth Street Baptist Church has a traditional look. The outside of the church is stone, and there is a large steeple. The basement and dining areas are downstairs, and the worship area is above street level."

*Warren St. (Ninth St.) Baptist Church detail (1872)

The coal chute on the southern side of the church attests to the building's age. Plantings of white and lavender flowers are also along the street side of the building, Ninth Street.

In his autobiography, Hughes writes, "My mother had often read papers at the Inter-State Literary Society, founded by my grandfather" (24). That society met at this church, on the second floor. His mother was a charter member of the group. No record remains of his grandfather's involvement, though he may have been part of the society. The church was a center of literary study as well as worship. Political topics were also discussed.

*Central School, now the 901 Building (1893)

This office building is the former Central School, which Langston Hughes attended in seventh grade. The top story has been removed. After classes, Hughes walked east a few blocks to the library, possibly, and to Massachusetts St. and downtown area jobs.

Hughes attended this school 1914-1915 until his grandmother died. His mother was in Lawrence in the fall of 1915 to settle her mother's affairs. She signed a bill of sale for 732 Alabama St. on Oct. 13, 1915. When Carrie and her second husband, Homer Clark, left for Illinois, Langston stayed on with Mary and James Reed, probably until the end of the fall semester. His mother and stepfather sent for Hughes to join them in Lincoln, where he continued school.

*Central School, 901 Kentucky, southwest corner, about 1895 (1893)

This is a view of Central School as it appeared when Langston Hughes attended junior high. Stonework and brickwork from the first and basement floors remain in the present-day building.

When the eighth grade teacher Ida Lyons seated Hughes and other African Americans in the back of the classroom, Hughes led his classmates in a successful protest (Armitage). John Taylor, one of those classmates, remembered this event when Hughes made a sign "Jim Crow Row." The students' parents and African American community leaders helped resolve the situation in favor of Hughes.

This photograph was taken by E.S. Tucker soon after its construction in 1893.

***Lawrence City Library, 200 West Ninth St., intersection of
Vermont and Ninth (1904)**

At a time when Lawrence movie houses and swimming pools excluded African
Americans, the library was open to everyone. Langston Hughes wrote that he
discovered the world of books in Lawrence. It is likely Hughes used this library.
He would have walked by the library, one block from Central School, on his
way to after-school jobs on Massachusetts St. and maybe Vermont St.

The 1904 Carnegie building served as the city library until 1972. It is on the
National Register of Historic Places.

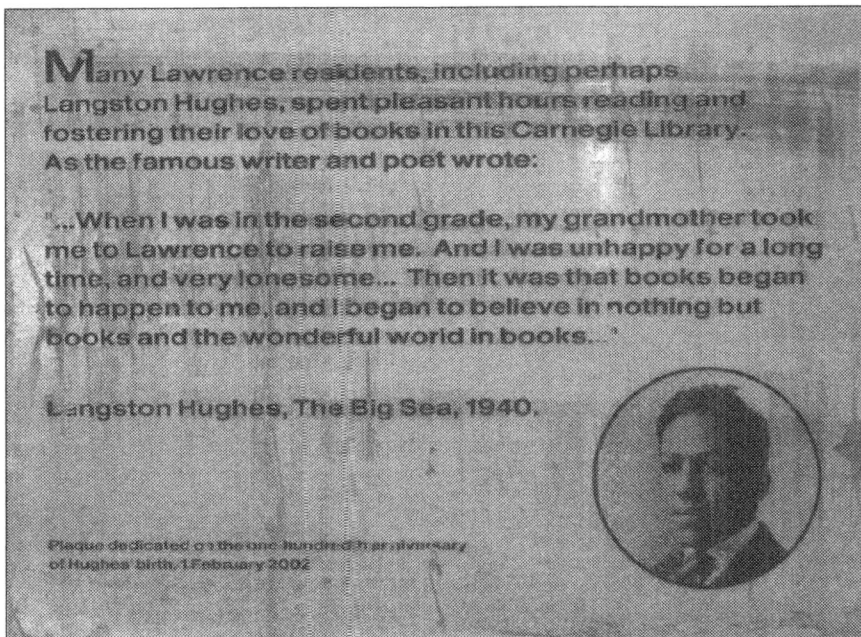

Many Lawrence residents, including perhaps Langston Hughes, spent pleasant hours reading and fostering their love of books in this Carnegie Library. As the famous writer and poet wrote:

"...When I was in the second grade, my grandmother took me to Lawrence to raise me. And I was unhappy for a long time, and very lonesome... Then it was that books began to happen to me, and I began to believe in nothing but books and the wonderful world in books..."

Langston Hughes, The Big Sea, 1940.

Plaque dedicated on the one hundredth anniversary of Hughes' birth, 1 February 2002

*Lawrence City Library, 200 West Ninth St. (1904)

This plaque, dedicated on the 100th anniversary of Langston Hughes's birth, is at the west entrance of the Carnegie building, once the City Library.

When Hughes lived with his mother in Topeka, they went to the library located on the Capitol grounds. He remembered, before six, appreciating the security and permanence of a library room (*Big Sea* 26).

Hughes does not mention the Lawrence library in particular. He wrote that he read "all of my mother's novels from the library" (*Big Sea* 26), although she then lived in Kansas City. The Hughes family apparently used library services throughout Hughes's childhood.

UNIVERSITY OF KANSAS

University of Kansas, about 1895

Langston Hughes's mother Carolina (Carrie) attended K.U. from 1894 to 1895, although she could not afford to be a full-time student. She took classes in English and German. This 1895 photograph (by E.S. Tucker) shows the extent of campus at that time. Most of the area outside downtown was treeless, since it was natural prairie.

This view shows Spooner Library on the left, the Physics Building in the distance, the Main Building, and Snow Hall on the right.

Hughes attended cultural events at K.U., as he writes in *I Wonder as I Wander*, "As a child in Lawrence, my grandmother had carried me to hear Booker T. Washington speak at the University of Kansas, so I had a vague memory of that great Negro educator and of the packed auditorium listening to him" (60). This event could have been around 1905 when Hughes was listed on the Kansas census as living with his grandmother.

Spencer Research Library, 1450 Poplar Lane (behind Strong Hall)

The special collections library of the University of Kansas includes a Langston Hughes Collection, a part of the Kansas Collection. Hughes donated most of the 300 items. It includes autographed books, letters, programs of his Kansas talks, and broadsides. The library contacted Hughes in the late 1950s for contributions. He generously responded through the rest of his life.

Visitors can see the range of Hughes's works in print media, including examples of music, poetry, drama, fiction, and prose.

The library is open 8 a.m. to 5 p.m., Monday through Friday, 785-864-4334.

Kansas Memorial Union, Thirteenth St. and Jayhawk Blvd. (1924)

Today, the Kansas Memorial Union is one of the distinctive buildings on the University of Kansas campus. The original 1924 building has been remodeled extensively, but the red brick material is original in some places.

Langston Hughes visited K.U. in 1932, 1958, and 1965. He saw "Auntie" Mary Reed in 1932 and also presented a K.U. poetry reading, sponsored by an African American sorority Alpha Kappa Alpha. He appeared at Fraser Hall (now demolished). Another sponsor was the Poetry Society. In 1932 his standard fee for readings was $100.00, although he would lower the fee if necessary (*I Wonder* 54).

In 1958, 1000 students attended his poetry reading here, with jazz band accompaniment. On his final visit to K.U., two years before his death, he presented a poetry reading in this building.

In 2002, the university and the Langston Hughes Society in Athens, Ga., sponsored an international conference to celebrate the one-hundred year anniversary of his birth. Alice Walker, Danny Glover, Robert Pinsky, Arnold Rampersad, Ossie Davis, Ruby Dee, Amira Baraka and others participated. Most of that conference took place here.

Snow Hall, University of Kansas (1886)

This building, dedicated in 1886, was razed in 1934. This was the biological science building, as it appeared about 1895 (photo by E.S. Tucker). Today, the new Snow Hall, built in 1930, houses the mathematics department.

Langston Hughes recalled watching medical students work with cadavers at K.U. He sneaked into the dissection room, and the young college students allowed him to stay (Rampersad V.1, 14). This is the building where anatomy and other training for medical students occurred.

McCook Athletic Field, University of Kansas, 1115 Illinois St.

Langston Hughes attended football games at this athletic field, near the location of the present stadium at Eleventh St. and Mississippi St. It was within walking distance of his grandmother's house. Hughes wrote that he attended games on Saturdays and could hear the students yelling (*Big Sea* 23). The crowd's roar is still audible throughout the campus area during football season. E.S. Tucker published this photograph in 1895.

EAST LAWRENCE AREA

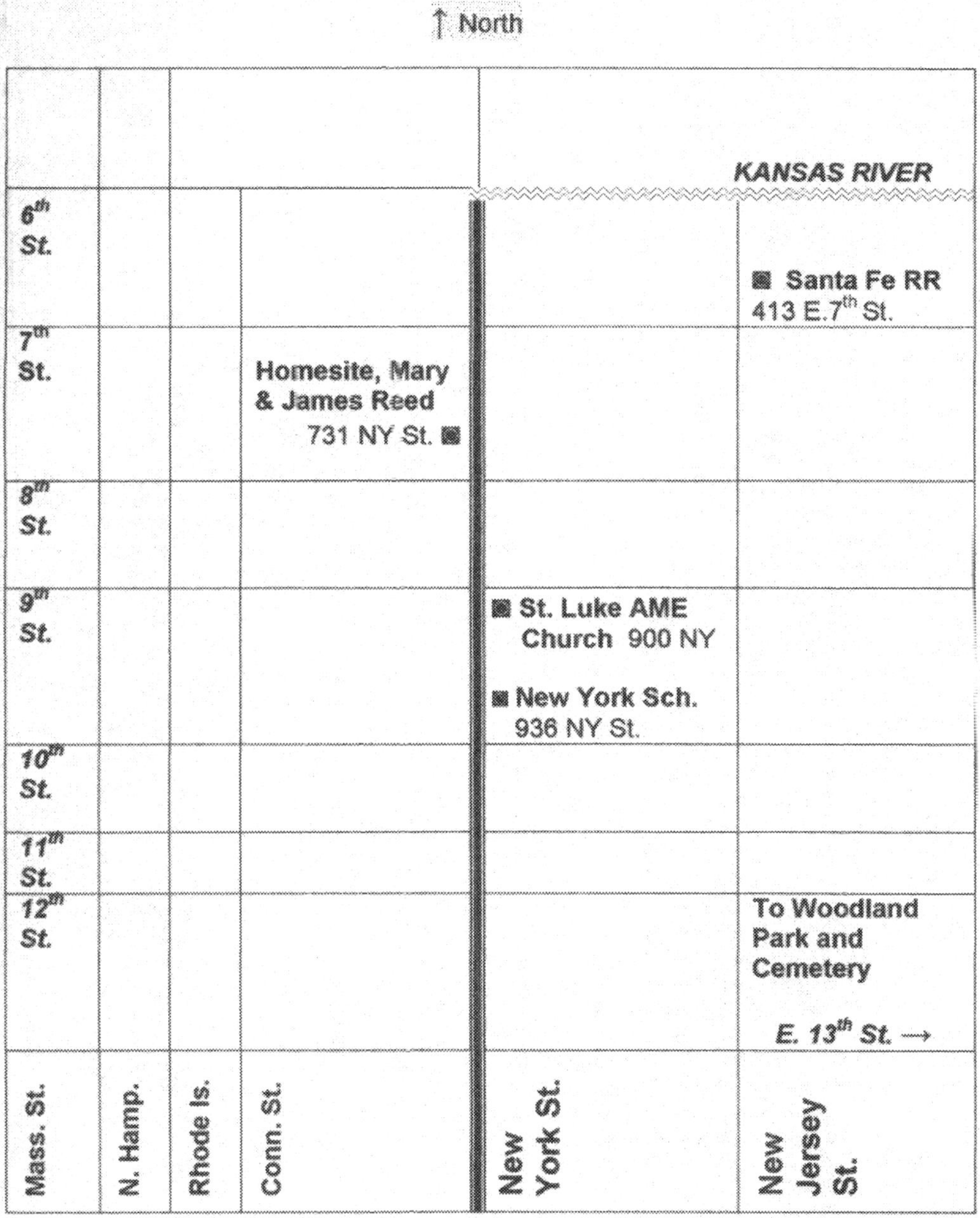

↑ North

KANSAS RIVER

6th St.

■ **Santa Fe RR**
413 E. 7th St.

7th St.

**Homesite, Mary
& James Reed**
731 NY St. ■

8th St.

9th St.

■ **St. Luke AME
Church 900 NY**

■ **New York Sch.**
936 NY St.

10th St.

11th St.

12th St.

**To Woodland
Park and
Cemetery**

E. 13th St. →

Mass. St.

N. Hamp.

Rhode Is.

Conn. St.

New York St.

New Jersey St.

Santa Fe (Amtrak) Railroad Station, Delaware and East 7th St.

When Langston Hughes lived with Mary and James Reed, he was a few blocks from the Kaw (Kansas) River and this railroad station.

This is not the original building, but the site is the same. Across the tracks to the left is the river. The foreground shows the original brick paving material from the 19th century. Several neighborhoods in East and Old West Lawrence have retained red-brick streets.

Santa Fe Railroad, 413 East Seventh St. (1882)

Langston Hughes saw this 1882 depot as a boy. The train company routed sixteen daily trains through Lawrence at the turn of the century.

Hughes's mother often worked in Kansas City and most likely would arrive and depart from here. When Hughes stayed at 731 New York St., he could walk here to greet her.

Hughes went to visit his mother on the train by himself. He learned to protect his money and later his passport, by pinning them inside his coat pocket "the way my grandmother used to tell me to do in order to protect my valuables when, as a child, she put me on the train in Lawrence to go visit my mother in Topeka or Kansas City" (*I Wonder* 190).

E.S. Tucker took this photo about 1895.

**Santa Fe (Amtrak) Railroad Station, 413 E. Seventh St.,
view looking East**

When Langston Hughes lived near this station, he writes of looking eastbound:

I used to walk down to the Santa Fe Station and stare at the railroad tracks, because the railroad tracks ran to Chicago, and Chicago was the biggest town in the world to me, much talked of by the people in Kansas. (Big Sea 17)

***St. Luke African Methodist Episcopal Church,
900 New York St. (1910)**

This Gothic revival building was built in 1910. The building was placed on the register of Kansas historical buildings in 2001 because of its connection to Langston Hughes. The congregation is applying for the National Register of Historic Places.

Hughes attended this church when he lived with Auntie and Uncle Reed, as he writes in his autobiography *The Big Sea*, "Auntie Reed was a Christian and made me go to church and Sunday school every Sunday" (18).

Hughes also remembers when Nash Walker, a famous Vaudeville performer from Lawrence, returned to this church to present "a concert at my aunt's church on the phonograph, playing records for the benefit of the church mortgage fund" (23). His uncle Nathaniel Langston, before he died, taught Nash music, and Hughes's mother was a schoolmate of Nash.

*Detail. St. Luke AME Church, 900 New York St. (1910)

The damaged corner stone indicates the church was founded in 1862 and rebuilt in 1910. St. Luke members have a tradition of connection to the Underground Railroad, an organization supporting slaves fleeing to freedom (Mathis).

In his autobiography Hughes describes a revival at the church, at which he was "saved from sin when I was going on thirteen. But not really saved." At that event he noted the "wonderful rhythmical sermons, all moans and shouts and lonely cries" (*Big Sea* 19). In 1960, Hughes credited the "Negro church" experience with inspiring his writing style (Mathis).

In his 1932 visit to Lawrence, Hughes attended church with his aunt, then remarried to Walter Campbell (Rampersad v.1 234). On Nov. 26, 1942, the Lawrence newspaper reported Hughes returned to St. Luke to present a poetry reading, assisted by a local singing group and a K.U. student (Appendix 3). According to the paper, his aunt, Mrs. Walter Campbell, was also present. He appeared in Kansas City and Topeka on the same trip.

New York Elementary School, 936 New York St.

When Langston Hughes and his grandmother lived with Mary and James Reed, he attended New York School, two blocks from their home.

In 1909, he lived down the street with the Reed family, according to the city directory, and perhaps he attended this school briefly. According to Katie Armitage, he attended New York School in the fourth to sixth grades (1913-1914) and "was remembered as a bright boy who sometimes spoke up in an independent manner."

Fred West, first African American principal in Lawrence, served here in 1896. By 1898, he was principal of Lincoln School.

This building, constructed in 1937, is not the original building, though it stands on the same site.

New York School, 936 New York St. (1869)

E.S. Tucker took this 1898 photo of the New York School building. Langston Hughes attended this school from fourth through sixth grades. The school and the neighborhood were integrated (Armitage). The city directory shows African Americans clustered together but living in mixed areas throughout town. However, schools often grouped African American students apart from others.

In his fictionalized novel about his childhood, Hughes wrote, "Sandy found the fifth-grade room upstairs and went in shyly" (*Not Without Laughter* 131-3). He described the African American students being seated in the back rows. "Sandy" (a boy similar to Hughes) won the boys' spelling contest and was interested in geography and science books.

Marker, home site of James and Mary Reed, 731 New York St.

This stone marks the former residence of Langston Hughes's grandmother's friends, James and Mary Reed. Hughes's grandmother Mary Langston would rent out her Alabama St. house and lodge temporarily with the Reeds.

In *The Big Sea*, Langston Hughes wrote: "Auntie Reed and her husband had a little house a block from the Kaw River near the railroad station" (17). Local citizens still call the Kansas River "the Kaw," an alternate spelling for the Siouan tribal name.

Hughes went on to describe how the Reeds raised chickens and cows at this rural site near the edge of town. He remembered Auntie Reed's cooking from the garden—peas and green onions—and fresh milk.

Mary and James Reed home site, 731 New York St.

Langston Hughes and his grandmother lived at this site occasionally, in a former house, and when his grandmother died, he moved back with the Reeds. Hughes's grandmother Mary Langston is listed at this address as a boarder in the 1908-09 and 1913-14 city directories.

The Reeds appear in city directories at this address from 1905 to 1923. James Wilson Reed worked as a laborer and as a sewer man for Kennedy Plumbing Co. Hughes remembered, "Uncle Reed dug ditches and laid sewer pipes for the city, and Auntie Reed sold milk and eggs to her neighbors" (*Big Sea* 18).

After James Reed died, Walter Campbell lived here, according to the city directory (1925-26), and he married Mary Reed, who owned this house (Rampersad V.1, 234). In March of 1932, his first visit to Lawrence since leaving in 1915, Hughes stayed with the Campbells at this site.

Left: 731 New York St.(?) Langston Hughes and James W. Reed (?)

This photograph of Langston Hughes may have been taken at 731 New York St., home of Mary and James W. Reed.

Hughes lived with the Reeds during the late fall of 1915, as he completed seventh grade at Central School. In this photograph, he does appear to be around age 13, consistent with other details. Hughes and the older man are dressed formally, for church, school, or some other daytime occasion. This could be James W. Reed, though he did not attend church, but rather "washed his overalls every Sunday morning (a grievous sin) in a big iron pot in the back yard, and then just sat and smoked his pipe under the grape arbor" (*Big Sea* 18).

729 New York St. Alley Barn

Langston Hughes wrote about James W. and Mary Reed raising milk cows and chickens on their 731 New York St. property. He remembered, "Auntie Reed let me set the hens, and Uncle Reed let me drive the cows to pasture" (*Big Sea* 18).

This barn dates from the time of the Reeds, and it is adjacent to the lot at 731 New York St., which is too small for a truck garden and farm animals. The Reeds' lot might have extended to this neighboring property, and this could be the Reeds' barn. The 1908-09 City directory shows no residence between 723 New York St. and 731 New York St., adding to the evidence. The Reeds may have owned a more extensive rural property as described by Hughes. The current owner agrees this was open land until the 1950s (Francisco).

The barn has hand-made bricks, hewn limestone, wooden barn doors and lintels, a chimney, ironwork, and other details that date it to the 19th century. The dutch door allowed circulation for livestock. It resembles other limestone structures in the Lawrence area that date to the 1860s (Marshall).

OAK HILL CEMETERY

**Oak Hill Cemetery, 1605 Oak Hill Ave. (intersection at
East Thirteenth St.)**

This 1895 photo by E.S. Tucker shows the entry to the cemetery, which has remains unchanged to the present day. Section 5, where graves of Langston
Hughes's grandparents are located, is to the right-hand side, toward the back
(eastern) edge of the cemetery.

The cemetery was founded in 1865 and expanded in 1876. It replaced Pio-
neer Cemetery (University of Kansas West Campus). Most of the Quantrill's
Raid victims were reburied here. A monument to them is in section 3.

Oak Hill Cemetery, 1605 Oak Hill Ave., section 5.

The small, ground-level stones at the left mark graves of Charles and Mary Langston, grandparents of Langston Hughes. Next to them are unmarked graves of their son Nathaniel Turner Langston (1870-1897) and Charles's son Desalines W. Langston, buried on October 30, 1931. Syble Langston, Nathaniel's daughter, according to county records, was buried at Oak Hill Cemetery in 1893, either here with the Langstons or with the mother's family, the Greggs.

The tilted stone in the right foreground is that of Rev. W. Mercer, pastor of the Warren (Ninth) St. Baptist Church from 1865 to 1885, during the lives of the Langstons.

Charles Langston, Marker, Oak Hill Cemetery

When Charles Langston died in 1892, he left his widow Mary to support their daughter Carolina (Carrie) Langston. His children Desalines and Nathaniel were adults by then. Langston Hughes never knew his grandfather.

Charles Langston attended Oberlin College, recruited African-American soldiers for Kansas regiments, worked for the Impartial Temperance movement, and taught at Quindaro Colored School in northeast Kansas. In the 1860s, Langston was part of abolitionist efforts that included the Underground Railroad in Ohio. He lived in Leavenworth, Kansas, 1862 to 1868 (Andreas V. 1, 350). He moved to the Lawrence area in 1870, where he farmed and worked in the grocery business at 820 Massachusetts St.

This granite stone was placed on the Oak Hill gravesite in 1991 by Pinckney School students.

Mary Sampson Patterson Langston, Marker, Oak Hill Cemetery

Mary Sampson Patterson first married Lewis Sheridan Leary, who was killed with John Brown at Harper's Ferry. Then she married Charles Langston in 1869.

Mary was born in North Carolina and educated at Oberlin College. In the 1860 U.S. Census, she is listed as a "milliner" in Oberlin.

She and Charles Langston married in 1869 and moved to a farm in Lakeview, Kansas, near Lawrence, in 1870. There she had two children, Nathaniel (1870) and Carolina (1873), Langston Hughes's mother. The family moved to town in 1886.

After her husband's death she supported herself and family by renting rooms in her house. Her grandson, Langston Hughes, lived with her much of his boyhood.

Hughes remembers her looking "very much like an Indian, copper-colored with long, black hair, just a little gray in places"(*The Big Sea* 12). He remembered her love of books.

Oak Hill Cemetery, Henry Copeland Gravestone

The name "H.E. Copeland" is engraved on the tree side of the white gravestone. Abolitionist Henry Copeland's brother John was hanged with John Brown in Virginia.

Henry was a nephew of Mary Langston's first husband Lewis Leary (Allen 3). He served as a first sergeant in the Colored Douglas Independent Battery. He also served with the U.S. Colored Light Artillery. After the Civil War, Copeland lived in Lawrence and worked as a carpenter until he died in 1895. He married Libby Miner on June 19, 1866, in Douglas County. He would have been a peer of Charles and Mary Langston.

Priscilla Gray marker, section 9 of Oak Hill Cemetery

The gravestone of African American Priscilla Gray is handmade with embedded seashells. According to Cathy Ambler, "Shells connect American blacks to African traditions where shells signify immortality" (*Historic Cemeteries*).

Though not a direct relative of the Langstons, the Gray family would have been part of the community at the time.

WOODLAND PARK

Woodland Park, Twelfth St. and Prairie Ave.

Woodland Park used to be north of Twelfth St. at Prairie Ave., east to Mount Cavalry Cemetery. The park included a half-mile race track and amusement park rides. This turn-of-the-century photograph shows throngs of people awaiting entry.

This is the site of one of the most notorious events in *Not Without Laughter,* the fictionalized autobiography by Langston Hughes. The park advertised a free day for all city children. It reniged in the paper the next day and requested African American children to stay away.

Hughes wrote of this event:

> *In the summer a new amusement park opened in Stanton, the first of its kind in the city, with a merry-go-round, a shoot-the-shoots, a Ferris wheel, a dance-hall, and a band-stand for weekend concerts. In order to help popularize the park, which was far on the north edge of town, the* Daily Leader *announced, under its auspices, what was called a Free Children's Day Party open to all the readers of the paper.* (195-6)

A corroboration of this account appeared in the *Lawrence Daily Journal World* of Aug. 17, 1910. The newspaper published an article announcing a city-wide free day at the park. However, it reported: "The Journal knows the colored children have no desire to attend a social event of this kind and that they will not want to go. This is purely a social affair and of course everyone in town knows what that means." Hughes would have been a boy of eight at this time.

**Brook Creek Park, Oak Hill Ave. and East Thirteenth St.,
near former site of Woodland Park**

According to city maps, all of the area formerly known as Woodland Park has
been combined with Brook Creek Park. The Brook Creek playground and pic-
nic area are just southwest of the historic amusement park.

From the Brook Creek Park sign, Oak Hill and Prairie Avenues converge at
Twelfth St., beside a paved circle and grassy area that were once a baseball diamond. This is the trailhead to the former Woodland Park.

Further east was a stop for the streetcars. The electric company, Lawrence
Light & Railway Co., owned the for-profit park, and streetcars provided service from Massachusetts Street (Knight). The widespread use of the automobile
led to the decline of both streetcars and the park. Streetcars ceased to run in
1933, when five bus routes replaced them.

The Park Hetzel family owned the Woodland Park land for many years after
Woodland Park days.

Woodland Park Entry, Prairie Ave. and Twelfth St.

This is the entry to the overgrown site of Woodland Park The open grassy area is where a baseball diamond was located in later years. Today, trails lead east into the riverside park, and the former site of Woodland Park rides is south of the main hiking trail. At the east end of the trail, a raised oval roadbed could be the former track for horse races.

This was an extensive site of amusement rides, bandstand, and concession buildings. During World War I, army troops bivouacked here. The Red Cross was housed in a park building during the war.

Woodland Park is almost completely forgotten, except for a few photographs and stories from Lawrence residents. Elfriede Fischer Rowe recalls expeditions to this park in *Wonderful Old Lawrence*.

Woodland Park, Prairie Ave. and Twelfth St.

This concrete footing was for the Daisy Dozer, a rollercoaster ride. It and several other footings are located south of the main trail, in dense undergrowth. Large masses of *vinca minor*, or periwinkle (above), suggest this area was landscaped in the past. Periwinkle is a domesticated plant and remains close to its original planting. The area was free of trees and brush at that time of the park, as seen in the old photographs.

Gary Marshall, who lived nearby, and his cousin, Donald Knight, remember abandoned wooden buildings and rides, but these were washed away in the 1951 flood.

Knight remembers the river further upstream, beyond Massachusetts St., was used for swimming, water skiing, and sunbathing in the 1940s and 1950s, and probably at the time of Woodland Park. This added to the stretch of the riverfront used for recreation.

Woodland Park Roller Coaster (about 1918)

The Daisy Dozer roller coaster was one of the notable rides at Woodland Park. This vintage photograph suggests the size of the park, which stretches along the riverbank for over a mile. County fairs used to set up in the area west of the park, according to Lawrence resident Gary Marshall, so fair goers could take advantage of the park facilities.

Concrete footings and some ceramic drainage pipes are the only remaining structures of Woodland Park.

Coins found at Woodland Park

Gary Marshall, who lived near the former site of Woodland Park in the 1940s and 1950s, found early 20ᵗʰ century coins at the park site, especially around a large, centrally located tree, which may have been a place for ticket sales. Marshall found the coins in the 1970s.

The coins include a 1906 liberty head dime, a 1900 V nickel, a rare 1866 liberty 3-cent coin, Mercury dimes (1919 and 1918), a 1903 liberty quarter, and a 1907 Indian head penny. The park began operation in 1909 with the advent of the electric car (Fagan), and these coins are consistent with that time period, with the exception of the rare old coin.

Marshall also found military insignia dated from the World War I era, when troops bivouacked at the park.

Keith Fellenstein took this photograph (2004).

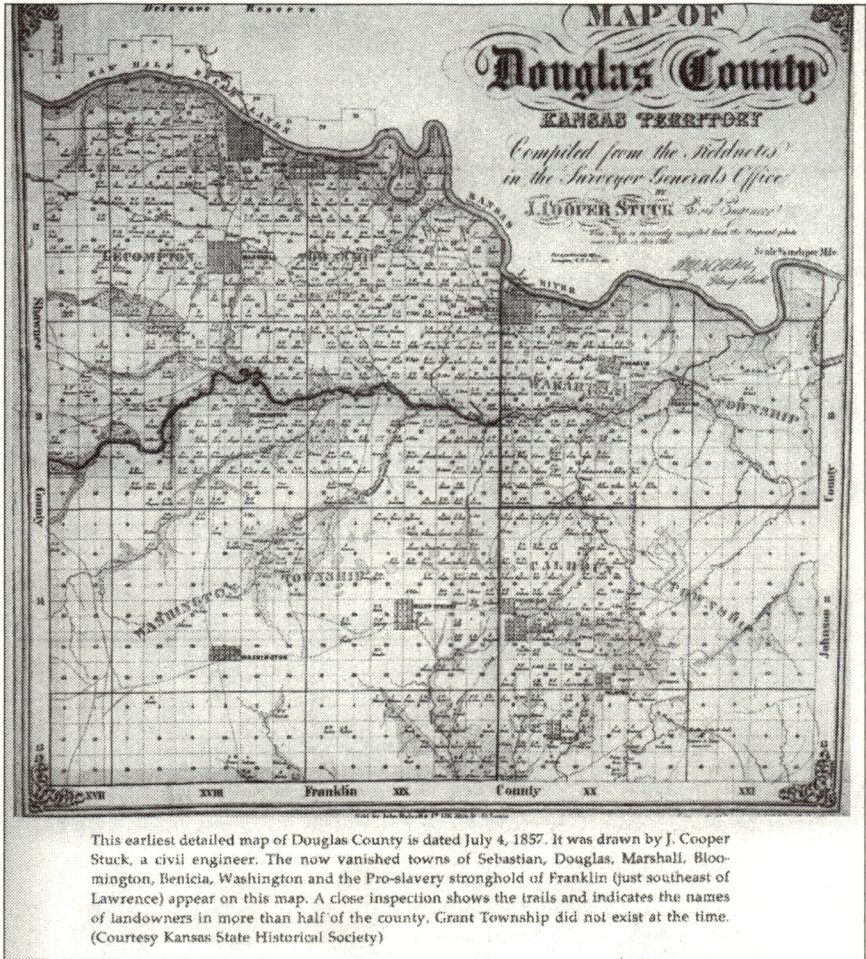

This earliest detailed map of Douglas County is dated July 4, 1857. It was drawn by J. Cooper Stuck, a civil engineer. The now vanished towns of Sebastian, Douglas, Marshall, Bloomington, Benicia, Washington and the Pro-slavery stronghold of Franklin (just southeast of Lawrence) appear on this map. A close inspection shows the trails and indicates the names of landowners in more than half of the county. Grant Township did not exist at the time. (Courtesy Kansas State Historical Society)

Map of Lakeview, 5.5 miles northwest of Lawrence

This 1857 map by J. Cooper Stuck shows the oxbow loop of the Kansas River, left of center, where the village of Lakeview stood. Charles and Mary Langston, grandparents of Langston Hughes, farmed near here in the late 19th century. Charles Langston owned section 16 of the Wakarusa township of Douglas Co., which runs to the south edge of the lake.

The flat floodplains of the Kansas River are among the most fertile soils in the world.

Lakeview, 5.5 miles northwest of Lawrence on Lakeview River Rd.

Lakeview is accessible by driving north on Iowa St. (Highway 59) past the 9th St. intersection; merging into the right-lane turnpike exit onto McDonald Dr.; turning left (west) at the Princeton St. light; and taking the first right (north) onto N. Iowa St., continuing until it runs into Lakeview Rd. Lakeview Rd. winds westward for five miles.

Charles and Mary Langston, lived at this site until 1886, when they moved to Lawrence. Perhaps the difficult winter between 1885 and 1886, as well as Charles's increasing age, led to the move. Langston Hughes's uncle, Nathaniel Turner Hughes, was born at Lakeview in 1870, and Hughes's mother, Carolina, was born here in 1873. Mary's mother Joanna Simpson lived here in 1880 (U.S. Census).

Charles Langston owned 122 acres along the south of the river. In the 1893-94 city directory, just after his death, Charles Langston is still listed as owning 26 acres of this land. He died in 1892, and in 1892 a private gun club was founded here. The private resort still owns the land.

Today the parts of the meander closest to the river have silted in, and a road bisects the loop, dividing the lake into two sections.

**Lakeview field, 5.5 miles northwest of Lawrence on
Scenic River Rd.**

This field just south of the Kansas River oxbow loop shows the soil fertility. The bottomland silt produces crops of hay, wheat, corn, soybeans, and other crops.

Charles and Mary Langston owned a farm near here from 1870 to about 1892. Charles was already in his fifties when he took up farming. The Langstons raised wheat, rye, corn, oats, Irish potatoes, and sweet potatoes. In 1883 A. T. Andreas observed, "[Langston] has one of the finest apple orchards in the State, and plenty of small fruit" (*History of the State of Kansas* V. 1, 350.). Andreas goes on to describe the farm: "It is all inclosed [sic] and all under cultivation except thirty acres of timber land. He has a comfortable residence and good farm buildings."

Lakeview School, 1908

This photograph from the Shane-Thompson Collection of the Kansas Collection at the University of Kansas shows a classroom about 20 years after the Charles and Mary Langston family moved away from Lakeview.

The one-room schoolhouses included all grades, with a limit of 60 students. Here the older students wear suits and ties. In this area the classes were integrated through all grades. Langston Hughes's mother and uncle probably attended this school.

From 1860 to 1877, Lakeview School was in a smaller building located north of the railroad tracks. In 1877, the brick and stone schoolhouse was built. An 1880 newspaper clipping describes a Lakeview school program of "songs, pantomimes, tableaus, recitations, orations, and dialogues" (Daniels 114). This may have been an inspiration for Carrie Langston's interest in theater.

JAMES LANGSTON MERCER HUGHES
FAMILY TREE

16 Henry CLAY
b. 14 Sep 1779
d.

8 Samuel CLAY
b. 3 Apr 1815
p. Bourbon Co., Ky.
m.
p.
d. 14 Feb 1888
p. Bourbon Co., Ky.

17 Margaret HELM
b. 24 Jun 1779
d. 1863

4 James Henry HUGHES
b. Unknown
p. Kentucky
m. Unknown
p.
d. 1887
p. Indiana

18 _____

9 ? (African Am.) HUGHES
b. Unknown
p. Kentucky
d. Unknown
p. Henry Co., Ky.

19 _____

2 James Nathaniel HUGHES
b. Sep 1871
p. Charlestown, Ind.
m. 30 Apr 1899
p. Guthrie, Okl.
d. Nov 1935
p. Mexico City

20 _____

10 Silas CUSHENBERRY/QUISENBERRY?
b. Unknown
p. Clark Co., Ky.
m.
p.
d. Unknown
p. Clark Co., Ky.

21 _____

5 ? CUSHENBERRY
b. Unknown
p. Clark Co., Ky.
d. Unknown
p. Indiana

22 _____

11 ? (African American)
b. Unknown
p. Clark Co., Ky.
d. Unknown
p. Clark Co., Ky.

23 _____

1 James Langston Mercer HUGHES
b. 1 Feb 1902
p. Joplin, Mo.
m.
p.
d. 22 May 1967
p. NYC
sp.

24 William QUARLES
b. 1731-1735
d. 2 Nov 1794

12 Capt. Ralph QUARLES
b. 1764
p. Spotsylvania Co., Va.
m.
p.
d. 1834
p. Louisa Co, Va.

25 Mary MILLS
b. 1740
d. 1779

6 Charles Howard LANGSTON
b. 1817
p. Fredericksburg, Va.
m. 18 Jan 1869
p. Elyria, Oh.
d. 24 Nov 1892
p. Lawrence, Ks.

26 ? AFRICAN AND AM. INDIAN
b. 1700s
d. 1700s

13 Lucy Jane LANGSTON
b. 1780?
p. Virginia
d. 1834
p. Louisa Co., Va.

27 ? POWHATAN WOMAN
b. 1700s

3 Carolina Mercer LANGSTON
b. 18 Jan 1873
p. Lakeview, Ks.
d. 3 Jun 1938
p. NYC

28 _____

14 James PATTERSON
b. Unknown
p. Fayetteville, N.C.?
m. 1835?
p.
d. Unknown
p. Unknown

29 _____

7 Mary Sampson PATTERSON
b. 1836
p. Fayetteville, N.C.
d. 8 Apr 1915
p. Lawrence, Ks.

30 ? FRENCH TRADER

15 Johanna/Joanna SAMPSON/SIMPSON
b. 1820
p. Fayetteville, N.C.
d. 1882-1885 ?
p. Lakeview, Ks. ?

31 ? CHEROKEE WOMAN

Genealogical Origins of
James Mercer Langston Hughes

Langston Hughes seldom referred to his ethnicity and family origins. In his autobiography *The Big Sea*, in a rare instance, he did describe his complicated identity: "You see, unfortunately, I am not black. There are lots of different kinds of blood in our family" (12). Hughes went on to list his ancestors as a Jewish slave trader, a Scots slave owner, an Englishman, a Frenchman, a Cherokee woman, and African Americans. A former teacher from Hughes's junior high days constructed the worst possible interpretation: "Did I tell you...he was a bad combination—part Indian, part Nigra [sic] and part white?"[1] Another source, a childhood friend named John Taylor, described how Hughes's mother was of Indian descent and both of his grandfathers were white, giving him "the appearance of a Spaniard." In the 1870 U.S. census, Hughes's maternal grandparents and uncles, living at Lakeview, Kansas, were listed as "white," but in the 1875 Kansas census, they were "Mulatto." When the family moved to Lawrence in the late 1880s, five miles away, city directories listed them as "colored." Hughes's ethnicity was not a simple matter.

Hughes's ancestry is only briefly mentioned in print. To most biographers, his life began when he was a leader of the Harlem Renaissance. And with limited print documentation, a genealogical tree for Hughes is difficult to construct. Although some of this information is available, it is usually incomplete and dispersed across several sources.

While his works speaks to higher causes—human dignity, personal freedom, and the abolition of slavery—Hughes's inconsistent experiences as a mixed-race youth in the Lawrence area form the basis of his art.

This information is collected from secondary sources in Lawrence and from biographies. While incomplete, this text presents as much as possible of Hughes's genealogy.

There are several branches in Hughes's lineage: the four grandparents—Sampson, Patterson, Langston, Hughes; Loise Leary, daughter of the Harper's Ferry martyr Lewis Leary and Hughes's grandmother; and the family of Hughes's stepfather, Homer Clark.

In pre-Civil War North Carolina, the homeland of the Learys and Sampsons, Hughes's ancestors lived as freeborn Blacks. In contrast, the Langston and Hughes branches originated within the plantation system—descendants of slave women and White slave owners in Virginia and Kentucky. All four of Hughes's direct lineages include White ancestry.

At least two of the families—Sampson and Langston—include American Indian ancestry. Hughes's grandmother Mary Sampson's grandmother was Cherokee Indian. Hughes's great-grandmother Lucy Langston was over one-half Indian, of an unknown tribe, possibly a coastal Powhatan Algonquin nation, the Pamunkey of Virginia (Rountree 174). Through her, Hughes gained another one-sixteenth Indian blood. Minimally, this indicates that Langston Hughes was one-eighth American Indian. At present time, some tribal nations would count this as enough ancestry for membership.

Charles and Mary Sampson Langston are buried in Oak Hill Cemetery, located on the east side of Lawrence, and this cemetery is a source for Hughes's genealogical background.

The Langston graves were unmarked until 1991, when Pinckney school children and a local funeral home identified and marked the gravesites. Still unmarked are the graves of Desalines W. Langston and Nathaniel T. Langston, uncles of Langston Hughes. Other prominent members of the African American community also rest there. So many Civil War era dignitaries are buried in Oak Hill Cemetery that newspaperman William Allen White called it the "Kansas Arlington" (Ambler, *Oak Hill Cemetery*). Most of the abolitionists murdered in 1863 by Quantrill's pro-slavery raiders are buried here.

Henry E. Copeland, a Civil War veteran, lies at Oak Hill. His brother John, a member of John Brown's Army of God, was hanged at Charleston, Virginia. Henry Copeland, inspired by his brother's martyrdom, served as the first sergeant in the Colored Douglas Independent Battery and the U.S. Colored Light Artillery (Rombeck 1B). Other well known nineteenth-century people buried at Oak Hill are John P. Usher, Lincoln's Secretary of Interior; James H. Lane, the first U.S. Senator from Kansas; Solon O. Thacher, one of the authors of the state constitution barring slavery; and Charles L. Robinson, a governor of Kansas in the early 1860s (Ambler, *Historic Cemeteries*).

Around 1895, the Oak Hill Cemetery was the site of a local memorial observance called Decoration Day. On this day Lawrence residents paid homage to the sacrifices made by other community members in their fight for the abolition of slavery.

The entrance of Oak Hill Cemetery is just beyond the Catholic cemetery, Mount Calvary. Many former residents of Franklin, Kansas, are buried there. Franklin was a pro-slavery community, located near Lawrence, but it no longer exists. The political and geographic boundaries of this area are as mixed as the people who settled here.

The Sampson (Simpson) Family

Langston Hughes's grandmother Mary Sampson (Patterson) Langston (1836–1915) familiarized him with their family ancestry through stories. It is probable that she did not elaborate at length upon that tangled genealogy, which began in North Carolina, or he would have commented more fully.

Mary Langston's grandmother was a Cherokee Indian, and her grandfather was a French trader (*Big Sea* 12). Sometime in the late-eighteenth century, they met on the banks of an unnamed river, perhaps as he traded goods. They spent enough time together to have at least two children, Langston Hughes's great-grandmother Johanna (or Joanna) and her sister Chloe. They shared the surname Sampson (or Simpson). Their Indian heritage allowed Johanna and Chloe to be classified as freeborn Blacks.

Johanna Sampson, Mary S. Langston's mother, lived in Fayetteville, North Carolina. Eventually, she met James Patterson, and they had a child, Mary. Patterson, a free African American man, was a stonemason, also from Fayetteville, North Carolina. Faith Berry's biography of Langston Hughes provides an alternate scenario. In that version, Mary was the ward of a well-to-do Black stonemason and his wife (8). More confusing is Benjamin Quarles's account of Mary's life—the surname Patterson results from her adoption by the John E. Pattersons of Cleveland when she was an infant (148-9). The guardian and the father may have been the same person. Variant stories demonstrate the difficulty in documenting African American heritages.

Further complicating the issue is the shift between the names "Sampson" and "Simpson." In the 1880 U.S. census, Johanna Sampson appears as "Joanna Simpson," a widow of 60 years, living on the Lakeview farm of "C.H. Langston." Her relationship to the head of the household is noted on the census as "mother-in-law." The document verifies Joanna Simpson's parents were both born in North Carolina.

Mary Sampson Patterson left her mother and North Carolina in 1857 after an attempt by slavers to kidnap and sell her into slavery. The entire nation was in an economic panic in the 1850s because of the speculation in Western lands. The South was especially affected. Under the prevailing pre-Civil War law, North Carolina classified her as a freeborn Black. The 1850 U.S. census reported 465 non-slave Blacks who lived in Fayetteville. This triracial community existed since colonial times (Libby et al. 1). Robert K. Thomas, in a report on Lumbee Indian origins, reviewed evidence from White sources. He found: "In Cumberland County, in the Fayetteville area around 1700, there were place names such as Indian Wells, Indian Walls, and Old Indian Stonehouse. In the late 1880's, Fayetteville absorbed an area including an Indian community of the same stock as the Lumbee" (70). Mary Sampson and perhaps also James Patterson could have had connections to this community.

Free men and women were relatively easy targets for freelance slavers to kidnap and then sell in other states. Under today's laws, Mary's ethnicity would be American Indian. None of this mattered to the slavers of the mid-1800s, since many American Indians were also enslaved. Mary's only recourse to avoid involuntary servitude was to flee her home. Mary Sampson Patterson left Fayetteville under the protection of respected White men. To travel freely, White men of property had to attest to her respectability.

She arrived in Oberlin, Ohio, in 1857 and entered a preparatory course at Oberlin College.[2] In 1858, she withdrew from Oberlin, perhaps because of her marriage to Lewis Leary. Leary was the father of the first of Mary's three children.

Mary and Lewis became conductors on the Underground Railroad. In 1859, Leary left his wife and daughter to join John Brown's Harper's Ferry raid, where he died.

In some accounts Mary gave birth to a daughter six months after Leary's death (Rampersad 6). In other accounts the child was already born (Quarles 148; Berry 2). Adding to the confusion is the uncertainty of the name. The 1860 Oberlin census lists the young widow Mary Leary as a "milliner" with a year-old child, "Lewis" Leary, and the child was incorrectly listed as a male. Her name appears in records spelled as "Lois" (Quarles 148-9), "Louise" (Berry 2) and "Loise" (Rampersad V.1 6). Perhaps the name was meant to be a feminine version of "Lewis," her father's first name.

Immediately after the death of Lewis Leary, that child, Loise Leary, became a central symbol of Oberlin's abolitionist movement (Quarles 148). When Mary re-married ten years later, 18 January 1869, the daughter was brought to Douglas County, Kansas, with her mother and her second husband Charles Howard Langston. She was part of the Charles Langston household in the 1870 and 1880 U.S. censuses. The 1875 Douglas County, Kansas, census lists "Lous. L. Lary," age 16, living with the "Langhston" family of C.H., Mary S., Deslines, N.[Nathaniel], and C.H. [Carolina]. She was employed as "hired girl," and she was from Ohio. This appears to be Loise Leary. James Redpath paid Lois' tuition at a private academy in Lawrence (Quarles 149, 221). Mary sent him regular reports about her academic and social progress.

Like his new wife, Langston appears to have brought a child to the marriage, Jean Jacques Dessalines (or Desalines or Desaline or D.W.) Langston (1859–October 1931).

Desalines W. Langston was born in Ohio and named after a Haitian revolutionary hero. He worked on the Langston farm at Lakeview, Kansas, in 1870 and 1875, according to census records. Desalines was married at least twice. A license is recorded in Douglas County, Kansas, on 27 March 1879, for the marriage of Desalines to Lizzie Maddox (*Douglas Co. Marriages* 173). James M. Hendry, Justice of the Peace, conducted the ceremony. The license records his name as "Desaline W. Langston." The 1880 U.S. census lists a "Lizzie Langston" living on the Lakeview farm, and this may be Desalines's wife.

Desalines moved from the farm to Lawrence before the rest of his family. He is listed in the 1883 Lawrence city directory as residing on New Jersey St. with Mrs. D.E. Langston. Perhaps the "E." represents "Elizabeth." The marriage to Lizzie Maddox must have ended, as county records indicate another marriage, between Desalines and Mary Thompson, on 8 January 1885.

When the Langstons moved to Lawrence, Desalines moved to a house on their property. In 1886, he lived next door to Charles and Mary Langston, at 726 Alabama St. He was employed as a barber. In August 1891 he and his wife lived in Topeka, Kansas. At the time of Charles's death, 1892, Desalines worked in a barbershop located on Charlotte Street in Kansas City, Missouri, and Hughes wrote of visiting this shop, and "an uncle of sorts" (*Big Sea* 304). Biographers usually refer to Desalines as Charles's foster son, though he may have been a child from a previous marriage. He died in Lawrence and was buried in Oak Hill Cemetery on 30 October 1931.

Mary Sampson Patterson Leary Langston died in Lawrence of "fecal impaction," a catchall diagnosis of the time (Rampersad V.1 19). She was buried at Oak Hill

Cemetery, beside Charles Howard Langston and between Desalines Langston and Nathaniel Turner Langston.

Mary Langston was a proud, determined woman. She was set in her ways and allowed nothing to get between her and her faith. Abolition was God's work and God would provide. Her main reading material was the Bible. Mary only sang biblical hymns, never any Negro spirituals, and absolutely never any popular songs. She had to have known that the nearby Warren Street Church sponsored gospel singing, and perhaps this is why she was not a regular participant (Butler "Church").

Mary Langston's daughter Carrie preferred plays and had aspirations to be an actress, although she had to make do with the local church's productions (*Big Sea* 25). She was artistic and became a trendsetter in Lawrence. She was one of the first of her peer group to cut her hair very short.

Mary Langston witnessed the decline of the Kansas abolitionist spirit in the early 20th century, as growing numbers of White immigrants arrived from southern states. When the African American community of Lawrence looked for a leader amidst changing conditions, Mary Langston turned to her abolitionist past.

A great source of pride was her status as the oldest living widow of the John Brown raiding party on the Harper's Ferry armory (Rampersad 13). Mary took Hughes on one of their few trips outside of Lawrence on 8 August 1910. They journeyed to Osawatomie, Kansas, to help inaugurate the John Brown Memorial Battlefield. Mary was given a seat of honor on the stage next to Theodore Roosevelt. It was a good time for the Langstons. The 1910 census declared their house at 732 Alabama Street was free of mortgage.

The Leary Family

Though Langston Hughes was not a direct descendant of the Leary family, his Aunt Loise Leary and other Leary relatives were part of his extended family. Loise Leary was half-sister to his mother, Carolina (Carrie) Mercer Langston.

Sally Revels was the matriarch of the Leary line (Libby et al. 2). Little about her is known. Reportedly, she was tri-racial, a mix of English and American Indian, maybe Croatan or Lumbee, and African (Quarles 87). She is remembered only because of her marriage to Jeremiah O'Leary.[3] He served in the Revolutionary Army under General Nathaniel Greene. This couple produced two 19th-century descendents, Lewis Sheridan Leary and John Anthony Copeland, Jr., who fought and died alongside John Brown.

Jeremiah and Sally O'Leary had a son named Mathew Leary, a freeborn Black, who married Julie Memriel. They lived in Fayetteville, North Carolina, where Mathew worked as a carpenter. This is the same community where Mary Sampson Patterson lived. They had at least four children: Lewis Sheridan, Henrietta, Henry, and Sara Jane. All of Mathew and Julie's children were freeborn.

Lewis Sheridan Leary (17 March 1835-18 October 1859) arrived in Oberlin, Ohio, in 1857. Although he had to work to help support his family, he enrolled in Oberlin College's preparatory course in the 1857-58 school year.

Oberlin became a central stop for fugitive slaves and a hotbed of abolitionism. The reason is simple; John Brown's father was a member of the Oberlin College board of trustees (Quarles 72). Young John Brown urged Leary and Copeland to join his father's war against slavery. Brown's interest in them resulted from a suggestion made by another prominent abolitionist, John M. Langston, Mary S. Patterson's future brother-in-law.

Lewis Leary was lionized as Oberlin's first recruit in John Brown's army. He was wounded on 10 October 1859 in the initial battle at Harper's Ferry. Without proper medical care, he suffered grievous pain for two days, before his death.

Lewis Leary's nephew, John Anthony Copeland, Jr. (8 August 1834-15 December 1859), was a freeborn African American, as were the rest of his family (Allen 3). He was born in Raleigh, North Carolina. His father, John Copeland, Sr., gathered their family and fled from North Carolina in 1842 (Quarles 88). They settled in Oberlin the same year. They had seven children. Little information exists about them except for Henry and John.

Henry E. Copeland (1840-1895) became a first sergeant in the Lawrence, Kansas, Colored Independent Battery detailed to the U. S Colored Light Artillery (Rombeck 4B). He is buried in Oak Hill Cemetery, section 9, in Lawrence. John, Jr., helped support his family; nonetheless, he was an Oberlin College preparatory student during the 1854-55 school year.

John Copeland was captured after riding with John Brown at Harper's Ferry. After a trial in Charles Town, Virginia, he was hanged on 16 December 1859.

The Langston Family

According to Langston Hughes in his autobiography, his mother's family, the Langstons, originated with the union of Lucy Jane Langston (d. April 1834) and Captain Ralph Quarles (d. 1834). The Virginia Quarles family traces their origin to Francis Quarles (1592-1644), an English poet. Francis Quarles lived at Romford, Essex. He married Ursula Woodgate and together they had eighteen children. Some of these emigrated to the colonies. The parents of Ralph Quarles were William Quarles and Mary Mills

Ralph Quarles, a wealthy plantation owner in Louisa County, Virginia, gained the rank of Captain in the America Revolution. Lucy Jane Langston was one of his slaves (Scott 2). She may have belonged to the Pamunkey Tribe, a member nation of the Powhatan Confederacy (Rountree 174). According to John Mercer Langston, Quarles accepted her as collateral for a loan (13). Since that was never paid back to him, she became his slave. She was mostly American Indian, with a small amount of African heritage. Her mother was also brought to the plantation. Lucy Langston's mother remained on the plantation until her death. Helen Rountree writes that "In 1787 a Pamunkey named John Langston owned and paid taxes on an adult slave (sex unrecorded) and three slave children, who disappear from his household thereafter. Lucy Langston's mother may have been one of these children" (174).

The name "Langston" appears associated with an "Indian" in a court document of 1691, in Henrico County, the location of the Powhatan Confederacy nations. A case brought before the levy court reads: "for wolves killed, Giles Webb (for Indian Langston)" (Henrico Co.249). Henrico County is almost adjacent to Louisa County, where Lucy Langston lived.

Lucy Langston had three children—William, Harriet, and Mary—from an unknown relationship. Quarles eventually emancipated all of them on April 1, 1806, in a declaration, which reads that Lucy and her heirs were free and clear of the "claims of all persons whatsoever" (Berry 2). Quarles and Langston had four other children: Maria, the eldest; Gideon Quarles, the eldest male; Charles Howard (Langston Hughes's grandfather); and John Mercer, the youngest (Scott 2). This appears to be the first occurrence of the name "Mercer" in the Langston family. It was used as a middle name for both Langston Hughes and his mother.

Upon his death, Quarles's estate went to Lucy and their three sons. However, Lucy died in 1834 from an unrelated illness. Quarles's eldest child, Maria, was not given anything from his estate. Quarles's will, dated 10 March 1834, is recorded in the Louisa County Registers Office:

> Ralph Quarles debts to be paid. To Gideon Langston, Charles Langston and John Langston the 3 youngest children of Lucy a woman I have emancipated 1 Apr 1806 all my lands lying on Hickory Creek with stock, etc. on that land to be equally di-

vided among them or land can be sold if they wish to buy elsewhere. Also to them all money I have at my death and money that is to come to me." (Book 9, page 109)

There is little information about Gideon Quarles Langston (1809-1855) (Scott 3). He enrolled in the 1834 fall semester at Oberlin College and earned an AB degree. Gideon moved to Cleveland, Ohio, where he owned livery stables. He died in Ohio of tuberculosis.

Charles Howard Langston's brother, John Mercer Langston (1829-15 Nov. 1897), was the most famous of Ralph Quarles and Lucy Jane Langston's three sons. John died in Washington, D. C., and was buried in Woodlawn Cemetery. Langston University, established in September 1897 near Guthrie, Oklahoma, was named after him.

John Langston enrolled in Oberlin College in 1849 at the age of 14, and he earned an AB, a Masters degree (1852), and graduated from Oberlin's theology seminary in 1853 (Oberlin 1-2). He entered the seminary as a preliminary to law school (Scott 3). According to William and Aimee Cheek, Langston applied at several law schools but was rejected because of racial discrimination. Stymied in his efforts, but even more determined to succeed, he found employment with Judge Philemon Bliss of Elyria, Ohio, as a junior clerk. Impressed with John Langston, Bliss tutored and trained him until 1854, when he passed the bar exam. He became Ohio's first African American attorney. Langston married another Oberlin graduate, Caroline M. Wall. Then James and Caroline moved to Brownhelm, Ohio. Caroline's father was a wealthy landowner in North Carolina. In 1855 James served on Brownhelm's City Council. In the 1860s, he became manager of Oberlin's school system.

As a professor of law, in 1868, John Langston reorganized the law department at Howard University in Washington, D. C. He later served as Howard's acting president. Finally, though, his candidacy for the permanent president's position was denied due to racial discrimination. For eight years, Langston served as the American minister and *charge d'affaires* to Santo Domingo. Langston, a delegate to the 1890 Republican State convention, won a seat to the Fifty-first Congress and served from September 23, 1890 to March 3, 1891. Besides his national reputation, John Mercer left the most offspring of the three brothers. He had at least seven children who attended Oberlin College.

A son of John Langston and Caroline Wall, Arthur Desaline Langston (August 1855-1908), earned a Bachelors of Arts degree from Oberlin in 1877 and a Master of Arts degree in 1886. He moved to St. Louis and became a well-known educator. On the Langston side, Langston Hughes was born into a prominent family.

Langston Hughes's grandfather Charles Howard Langston, known to his admirers as Colonel, was born 31 Aug. 1817 in Fredericksburg, Virginia (Andreas v. 1, 350). His parents moved to Louisa County soon after his birth, until he was fifteen. At their deaths, he and his brothers relocated to Oberlin, Ohio, where they attended college. At the start of the Civil War, Charles moved to Illinois and recruited Black troops for the 54th and 55th Massachusetts Regiments (Scott 3). Charles did not enlist. He moved to Leavenworth, Kansas, in 1862 and lived there until 1868.

The move to formally integrate African Americans into Leavenworth began when community leaders held a meeting on 5 February 1862 to discuss ways to accomplish their integration. Charles became an active leader within a few months. He was described, at that time, as a free "Mulatto" Leavenworth schoolteacher (Sheridan, "From Slavery," 171).

Many Kansas Republicans did not want universal suffrage in the 1860s. They were afraid that if Kansas did have universal suffrage, the state would be flooded with Blacks wanting to vote (Sheridan 4). Langston shocked them in 1863 by arguing that all racial qualifications for suffrage should be eliminated.

According to Sheridan, in the mid-1860s, he was described in the newspapers as a prominent Kansas City attorney. On February 10, 1867, he argued that any collateral consideration of sex discrimination was absolutely incompatible with the issue of Negro suffrage. By arguing in favor of this position, he divided the women's movement from the abolitionist movement.

During this period his first wife (birth and death information unknown) died (Scott 3). Perhaps she was the mother of Desalines Langston. Charles returned to Elyria, Ohio, and courted Mary Sampson Patterson Leary, the widow of Lewis Leary. The bride had a daughter from her previous marriage, Loise Leary. Before Reverend Kenyon, they married on January 18, 1869. After this marriage, in 1870, Charles Langston's family—Desalines, Mary, and Lois Leary—moved to a 122-acre farm near the tiny community of Lakeview, Kansas. Their farm was situated along the bottom arc of a U-shaped oxbow in the Kansas River, five miles upstream from Lawrence (see map, page 74 of this volume).

The Lakeview farm was a prosperous household of hired help and relatives. The 1870 U.S. census showed Joanna Calvin, Leonard Peter, Samuel Davis, Lois "Lears" or "Learo," as well as Charles, Mary, Desalines, and Nathaniel Langston at

Lakeview. The real estate and personal property values came to over $8000. Mary's children Nathaniel Turner Langston and Carolina (Carrie) Mercer Langston were born at Lakeview. Carrie was the mother of poet Langston Hughes.

In 1875, the Kansas Census showed Charles, Mary, Desalines, Nathaniel, and Carrie Langston in residence at the farm, along with "Lous. Lary" (Loise Leary) and David Lightfoot, listed as "farm help." In 1880, the census shows a household of Charles, Mary, Caroline, Nathaniel, and Lizzie Langston, along with Joanna Simpson, listed as the mother-in-law, and John Sheas, a servant.

Although he was over fifty when he bought the Lakeview property, Langston was a successful farmer. In 1883 A. T. Andreas observed: "[Langston] has one of the finest apple orchards in the State, and plenty of small fruit." (*History of the State of Kansas*). Andreas goes on to describe the farm: "It is all inclosed [sic] and all under cultivation except thirty acres of timber land. He has a comfortable residence and good farm buildings" (v. 1, 350).

For the Langston family, early life in Kansas was good. Charles became prominent for his stands as Kansas was debating African American suffrage. Black-owned newspapers gave him extensive coverage and accurately quoted his impromptu speeches. At the same time, the April 21, 1879, edition of the *Colored Citizen* supported his suffrage movement when they printed his calculated musings: "I want to see Kansas as black as midnight rather than have to endure any more racial inequality" (quoted in Sheridan). Although his own political and social popularity was at an all-time high, Kansas's statutes allowed racial discrimination to occur in public institutions. When he, described as a prominent Lawrence attorney in the papers, and an African American lawmaker were denied service at an ice-cream counter in 1881, Langston's accusatory response reassured his constituency that he would soon make things better.

In Lawrence, where the survivors of Quantrill's Raid were heroes, the Langston family belonged to the social elite. Their comings and goings were reported in the gossip columns. On 21 March 1884, Charles and Mary attended one of the area's largest social events of the season "...for coloreds...."[4] Almost two-hundred people gathered at the home of Deacon Alexander Gregg and his wife to help them celebrate their 25th wedding anniversary. The newspaper reported that Charles and other men presented the couple with a fine silver water pitcher. Mary and other women gave them a silver cake tray and a silver goblet.

Two years later, according to the city directory, Charles, and presumably his family also, moved into Lawrence at 732 Alabama Street. His move to town came after the severe winter of 1885-6, which could have affected his orchard. In Lawrence he became a business associate of Richard Burns in a grocery store located at 820 Massachusetts Street. Charles belonged to a fraternal order that met at 910 Massachusetts Street. In 1890 he was the secretary for the Colored Masons Western Star No 1. He continued to farm on twenty acres, according to the city directory (1893). When he died in 1892, however, he left financial debts for the family.

Nathaniel Turner Langston (1870–April 1897) was born at the Lakeview farm. He was named after Charles's hero, General Nathanial Turner, the leader of an 1831 slave revolt in Virginia. In 1893, he lived with his mother at 732 Alabama St. and worked in his father's grocery business, Burns & Co. Nathaniel married Nellie Gregg on 20 February 1893. Nellie Gregg was the ninth of eleven children by Deacon Alexander Gregg (b. 20 March 1824) and his third wife, whose twenty-fifth wedding anniversary was celebrated in Lawrence. Born in Kentucky to a slave mother and a White slaveholder, Gregg also had been emancipated from slavery and was a community leader. The marriage joined two prominent families. In the 1895 Kansas Census, Nathaniel was a "printer."

Nathaniel Langston died in a mill accident in Lawrence and was buried at Oak Hill Cemetery on 1 May 1897. Some sources argue that Nathaniel actually died of consumption. Either cause of death seems reasonable. In July of 1898, Nellie Langston buried a child, Syble Langston, 18 months old, in Oak Hill Cemetery, most likely Nathaniel's daughter.

Carolina "Carrie" Langston was born 18 Jan. 1873 on the Lakeview farm. In April of 1894, she finished a ten-week course in kindergarten and primary school teaching at the Kansas State Normal School in Emporia, Kansas, as Mercer Langston (Rampersad 9). When the fall 1894 semester began, she enrolled at the University of Kansas in Lawrence. She took one German class and one English class. Money problems, however, forced her to withdraw from the university in 1895. That same year, her mother Mary S. Langston mortgaged their property at 726 Alabama St. (Appendix 2). Eventually, all of the Langston property—the Lakeview farm, the house at 726, and the 732 Alabama St. house—were lost.

According to the 1896 Lawrence city directory, Carrie Langston was working as deputy clerk for the Douglas County court. She left Kansas to pursue a teaching career in Indian Territory, now Oklahoma (Rampersad 9). She married James Nathaniel Hughes in Guthrie, Oklahoma, in 1899, and the couple moved to Joplin, Missouri. After their separation, Carrie continued to work in the northeast Kansas area, including a year as a stenographer in Topeka, until she married Homer Clark, her second husband.

Doctors told Carrie Langston as early as 1935 of a cancerous lump in her breast. Dismissive of any future operations to excise the tumor, she resigned herself and those around her to death. She died of breast cancer in Harlem on 3 June 1938.

The Hughes Family

The printed materials at Langston Hughes's May, 1967, memorial service gave his full, legal name as "James Mercer Langston Hughes." Biographer Faith Berry asserts that not only did he actually prefer this full version of his name, but it was his legal name. This can not be checked against his birth records. Until 1910, the local government of Missouri's Jasper County did not require any birth and death registration from its residents. He did descend from a distinguished family on his father's Hughes side.

Hughes's grandfather was James Henry Hughes (d.1887), a veteran of the Civil War. James H. and his wife were both born into slavery, in Kentucky. After the Emancipation Proclamation, they moved to Indiana. They lived the rest of their lives there and were buried in Indiana. James H. had two brothers who joined the U.S. Cavalry and served as Buffalo Solders, though their exact names are unknown (Rampersad 10).

Other Hughes relatives lived in Douglas County, Kansas, also, in Clinton township. Marinda Hughes appears in the 1870 U.S. census, Clinton Township, as the wife of Joseph Simpson, with two small children, John and Joseph. She was reputedly a sister to James H. Hughes. Patrick Simpson, also of Clinton, was married to Melissa Simpson in the same census, and their origins are Kentucky, like the Hughes family. The Simpson family has an oral tradition that Marinda was a runaway slave originally from Kentucky (AfriGeneas Forum), and she fled to Missouri. Melissa and Patrick Simpson, who are a generation older, also went from Kentucky to Missouri before arriving in Kansas, and Melissa may be the sister (1875 Douglas County census). Freed and escaped slaves settled in the Wakarusa River valley in Douglas County, Kansas (Parker 4). Johanna Sampson, Mary Langston's mother, was also known as Joanna Simpson (1880 US Census), and she may have been distantly related to the Kentucky Simpsons.

James Hughes's wife's mother was an unidentified plantation slave. His wife's father, Silas Cushenberry (alternately spelled Quisenberry), an Englishman, lived in Ashland, Kentucky, and worked as a slave trader in Clark County (Hughes *Big Sea* 11).

James Hughes's father was Samuel Clay, a whiskey maker, and his mother was a slave. Langston Hughes remembers his grandfather as "Sam Clay, a distiller of Scotch descent, living in Henry County" (*Big Sea* 12). The 1860 census shows Samuel Clay, age 45, living in nearby Bourbon County, not Henry County, with assets of $163,200. No other Samuel Clay lived in Kentucky at this time.

James H. Hughes and his wife had at least three children. Langston's father, James Nathaniel Hughes, was born in Charlestown, Indiana (Sept. 1871), and he died Nov. 1934. According to Rampersad, there are at least two other siblings: a sister, Sarita (Sallie) J. Hughes (d. 1935), and the younger brother John S. Hughes. The brothers James and John moved west during the 1898 Homestead Settlement to buy land in the Oklahoma Territory. James had a 160-acre homestead. John invested all of his money in land. After oil was discovered, he leased his Oklahoma mineral rights to others, moved to Los Angles, bought California real estate, and there accumulated more assets. John never married. Langston and he had a close relationship. A measure of this closeness is contained in a promise he made to John, to bury him near the rural Indiana farm of his youth.

James Nathaniel Hughes's sister, Sarita J. Hughes, married Sam Garvin. They lived in Indianapolis, Indiana (Rampersad 11).

Another Hughes cousin, Flora D. Coates, was known, but her parentage was not clear. She appeared to be one of James's nieces or the child of a sibling's spouse. Hughes dedicated his 1931 book *Selected Poems,* published by Knopf, to her.

James Nathaniel Hughes was Carrie's first husband (Rampersad 11). They met in Guthrie, Oklahoma, where Carrie moved in 1895 to teach grammar school. James N. Hughes lived in Langston township, Oklahoma, where he was a storekeeper, but he wanted to practice law. They were married 30 April 1899 in Guthrie, Oklahoma, by Judge J. L. Foster of the Probate Court. They moved from Guthrie to Joplin, Missouri. Carrie's mother Mary joined them.

They had a child soon after their marriage. Unfortunately, their new baby, a male infant, died at or near his birth in Joplin, Missouri (1900). Langston Hughes knew nothing of this child until 1958, when Max Baird of the University of Missouri faculty told him of this research. In 1901, Carrie, pregnant again, visited James's younger brother John in St Louis. Shortly after this trip, on 1 Feb. 1902,

Langston Hughes was born at 1602 Missouri Street in Joplin. Carrie, James, and the infant moved to a larger house at 1046 Joplin Ave. with Mary Langston shortly after the birth. However, by 29 Oct. 1903, James Hughes relocated to Mexico. Carrie, Mary, and Langston returned to 732 Alabama St. in Lawrence, where they appear in the 1902-03 city directory.

In 1907, Mary, Carrie, and the boy Langston joined James Hughes in Mexico, to attempt reconciliation. An earthquake that occurred on April 17 of that year scared them into returning immediately to the U. S. The date of the divorce is unknown. In 1908 Carrie and Langston Hughes lived in Topeka, where she worked for an African American attorney (*Big Sea* 26). Carrie took her child to the library and started his life-long love of books. In Mexico, James Hughes married his German housekeeper, Bertha Klatte (1923). He died in 1934 and was buried in the Panteon Moderno, Mexico City, Mexico.

Uncle John Hughes continued to live in Los Angles until he entered a nursing home in 1967. This was a bad year for the Hughes family. On 6 May 1967, Langston Hughes went to the emergency room at the New York Polyclinic on West 50th Street in extreme pain. He died at 10:40 on 22 May 1967. The cause of death was septic shock due to bacteremia in prostate tissue. His last trip to Lawrence, Kansas, where he spent so much of his youth, was in 1965.

The Clark Family

The family of Langston Hughes's stepfather, Homer S. Clark, had an influence on his teen years and adulthood. Homer was a cook from Topeka, and he became Carrie's second husband in 1915. Clark's mother was a prominent church member in Topeka. He had a son named Gwyn "Kit" Shannon Clark from a relationship that occurred prior to his marriage to Carrie. The marriage of Homer and Carrie produced no children. Complicating a genealogy of the Clark family, for reasons known only to herself, Carrie often spelled "Clark" as "Clarke."

While the following record of their married life is incomplete, it illustrates the changing social patterns confronting the Clark family. Hughes notes in his autobiography, aptly titled *I Wonder as I Wander,* his pattern of constant movement: "I belonged to a family that was always moving" (57). The following account of his travels is from his autobiographies and Rampersad's biography:

After the death of Mary S. P. Langston in April of 1915, the new blended family of Homer, Carrie, Kit, and Langston shared the house at 732 Alabama Street, according to the 1915 city directory. After signing the bill of sale with

Carrie on 15 October 1915 (Appendix 2), Homer left Lawrence to seek employment. Carrie and Kit then left to join Homer, leaving Langston with family friends, the Reeds. Carrie sent for Hughes to come live with them in Lincoln, Illinois, at the end of 1915. Lincoln was once a stop on the Underground Railroad, and it was in Lincoln that Hughes first wrote verse. On the last day of the school year, Homer left the family and moved to Cleveland to look for a job. At summer's end, the rest of the family left Lincoln and joined Homer in Cleveland.

In Cleveland, the four lived together at 11217 Ashbury Avenue until 1917, when Homer left for Chicago. Carrie and Kit soon joined him. Hughes stayed in Cleveland and moved into his own apartment at 2266 E 86th Street. Homer left Chicago shortly after Carrie and Kit joined him. In the spring of 1919, Carrie and Kit moved back to Cleveland, where they lived at 5709 Longfellow Avenue.

Next, the family tried Washington, D.C. In November 1924, Langston family was invited to stay with wealthy Langston relatives in Washington, but when he arrived, he found Homer already had moved out and Carrie reconsidering her decision to live with John Mercer Langston's descendents. Hughes, working in a laundry one day, looked up and saw his mother in tears with Kit in tow. Embarrassed by her low status, she left the comfort of the LeDroit Park cousins' home for the city's slums. This and similar experiences soured Hughes on the African American upper class. Hughes, Carrie, and Kit moved into a two-room, apartment at 1749 S Street. Hughes had enough of Washington D. C. and left in February, 1926.

In Atlantic City, New Jersey, Langston Hughes spent Christmas of 1926 with Carrie and Kit. Hughes and Homer were in Atlantic City at Thanksgiving of 1929. The 1930 U.S. census shows Langston Hughes as a roomer in Westfield, New Jersey. After several more moves, Carrie and Kit lived in Cleveland again, as Langston traveled.

Patrons helped the family through the Depression. The grandson of a wealthy banker subsidized Hughes's writing for a year after his return from the Soviet Union. Noël Sullivan also sent Carrie money in the darkest months of the Great Depression. In October of 1935, Kit left Carrie and joined the Civilian Conservation Corps. During this time period, Carrie found out that she had breast cancer. Carrie, Kit, Hughes, and two of their distant cousins spent Thanksgiving, 1935, in Oberlin, Ohio. The next spring, Carrie, Kit and Hughes lived at 2245 E 80th Street in the same building that Hughes lived in while attending high school. The cramped apartment forced another move to 2256 E 86th Street, where the three of them lived until 1936.

The year 1936 was unfortunate for the Clarks. In November, a clerk in a Cleveland store assaulted Carrie. She wanted to return a fur coat, but the clerk would not accept it since she had it longer than their return policy allowed. Words were exchanged, then physical blows. The same year Kit entered Bellevue Hospital for treatment of alcoholism. He fell asleep while drunk and set his mattress on fire. He escaped serious injury. Alcoholism prevented Kit from working or from attending embalming school, though Hughes sent him money. Often drunk, Kit worked himself up into a rage and abused Hughes (Rampersad V.1 150). There was no discernable reason for this treatment, other than Hughes was a success and Kit was a failure. Nonetheless, Hughes remained loyal to his stepbrother. Hughes's book *Dream Keeper* (1932) is dedicated to Kit. In 1937 Hughes wrote his first will as a correspondent in the Spanish Civil War. He provided a trust fund to pay for the education of Kit's children. He sent Kit money for Willberforce College in Ohio in the spring and fall semester of 1937, but he flunked out both semesters.

Carrie lived in Cleveland again in 1938. In June of 1939, Kit sublet Hughes's apartment at 66 St Nicholas Place in Harlem. Kit spent this time in uncontrolled drinking. As a result, in 1941 Hughes was evicted from his apartment. Kit was $98.00 behind in the rent. Hughes was in the hospital and friends had to retrieve his belongings.

Kit was a father when he enlisted in the army December of 1942. He married a woman named Norma and had five children: Carroll, Langston, Calvin, Maceo, and Gwendolyn. Hughes maintained contact with Kit's wife Norma, although his relationship with Kit was strained. When Gwendolyn married in 1964, Hughes wrote that she was the most beautiful bride that he had ever seen.

Hughes also stayed in contact with Carroll. That relationship was especially problematic. As a teen, Carroll was a frequent visitor to Hughes's residence. Affected by the social turmoil of 1960s, he changed his name to Carroll X to express his discontent as a Black radical. In February of 1967, Carroll was fresh out of jail, broke, and needing a loan from Hughes. A little later he seemed to get better. He found a job and bought a car. Soon, however, he was reported missing by his family. After a few days, the California police found his abandoned car. When the trunk was forced open, they discovered his body stuffed inside. This tragedy occurred just a few months before Hughes's own death.

The Clark family seemed to restore Langston Hughes's sense of family. Hughes considered Homer as his dad.[5] His own father, James Hughes, he called "Father."

As an adult he became closer with his uncle John Langston and cousins Sallie Garvin and Flora D. Coates.

The vicissitudes of the Clark and Hughes families show the impact of social changes. The first new reality was that the old Underground Railroad towns were becoming meaner places. According to the biographer Rampersad, Hughes blamed this situation on an influx of African American populations in these places. New populations of Whites, ones who had not played a part in the abolition of slavery, moved into these areas also. Small, integrated towns transformed into segregated municipalities. Topeka, Lawrence, Lincoln, Chicago, and Cleveland experienced the same population shift. Only Oberlin seemed immune.

The second new reality was a widespread economic instability that resulted from the disbanding of the Freedmen's Bureau and other such organizations. These groups had provided economic and moral support to African Americans. This economic instability eroded the structure of families. These new realities were reflected by the struggles of the Clark family of Langston Hughes as they moved from city to city.

As Hughes gained prominence, he returned to Kansas periodically to visit old friends and relatives (Appendix 3). He performed poetry readings at the University of Kansas in 1932, 1957, and 1965. He appeared in Kansas City in 1939 and in Topeka and Lawrence in 1942. He maintained ties with "old friends and relatives," as noted in the *Kansas City Star* (5 April 1939). When he traveled the country, he opened his performances with the words, "I was born in Missouri, …I grew up in Kansas in the geographical heart of the country, and [am] therefore, very American" (*Wonder* 57).

[1] Paulette D. Sutton interviewed Ida Lyons, Hughes's old English teacher at Central Junior High School, in Lawrence, Kansas, on 10 April 1972. The full quotation is found in Sutton's *Langston in Lawrence*, p. 24, an unpublished manuscript at the Lawrence Public Library.

[2] Oberlin information is from Leslie H. Fishel and Benjamin Quarles and Quarles, *Allies for Freedom*, 87.

[3] Arnold Rampersad, Faith Berry, and Benjamin Quarles all spell Leary without an "O."

[4] On page 182, according to the *Douglas County, Kansas Genealogy Society* (1989), *The Western Recorder* of Lawrence, Kansas, reported that this was a silver anniversary for "coloreds." Nevertheless, except for that single remark, the newspaper reported this party as one of the community's notable social events. Their article included a detailed itemization of the many fine silver presents. The donors' names were prominently displayed and seemingly correctly spelled. Among the other local papers, such as the *Lawrence Journal World Daily*, only the largest

and most exclusive African American social events were reported in a brief, objective manner, and those items would never appear in the society pages. Items of interest to African Americans were randomly placed throughout the paper.

⁵ "But Kit and I almost lost the battle when Dad's own mother arrived for a visit from Topeka," writes Hughes in his autobiography *The Big Sea* (135).

Works Cited

1860 U.S. Census. http://www.oberlin.edu/external/EOG/1860census/K-L.htm>. Last update 28 May 2004. Last visit 9/7/2004. Other census figures are from U.S. and state archives.

1883 Lawrence City Directory. Lawrence: Lawrence Pub. Co., 1883.

1886 Lawrence City Directory. Lawrence: P.T. Foley, 1886.

1888 Green & Foley's Lawrence City Directory. Lawrence: Green & Foley, 1888.

1890–91 Lawrence City Directory. St. Louis: Benson Bros., 1890.

1893–94 Directory of the City of Lawrence and Douglas County. Wichita: Leader Directory Co., 1893.

1896 Hoye's City Directory of Lawrence, Kansas. Kansas City: Hoye, 1896.

1898 Chittenden's Lawrence City Directory. Vol. 4. St. Louis: Chittenden Directory Co., 1898.

1900-01 Chittenden's Lawrence and Douglas County, Kansas Directory. Vol. 5. St. Louis: Chittenden Directory Co., 1900.

1902–03 Chittenden's Lawrence and Douglas County, Kansas Directory. Vol. 6. St. Louis: Chittenden Directory Co., 1902

1905 Polk's Lawrence City Directory. Sioux City: R. L. Polk, 1905.

1907 Polk's Lawrence City Directory. Sioux City: R. L. Polk, 1907.

1909 Polk's Lawrence City Directory. Sioux City: R.L. Polk, 1909.

1911 Polk's Lawrence City Directory. Sioux City: R. L. Polk, 1911.

1913–14 Polk's Lawrence City Directory. Sioux City: R. L. Polk, 1913.

1915 Polk's Lawrence City Directory. Sioux City: R. L. Polk, 1915.

1917 Polk's Lawrence City Directory. Sioux City: R. L. Polk, 1917.

1919 Polk's Lawrence City Directory. Sioux City: R. L. Polk 1919.

1923 Dunham's City Directory, Lawrence, Kansas. Springfield, Mo.: Dunham, 1923.

1925–26 Polk's Lawrence City Directory. Kansas City, Mo.: R.L. Polk, 1925.

Adams, Virginia, Katie Armitage, Donna Butler, Carol Shankel, and Barbara Watkins, compilers. *On the Hill: A Photographic History of the University of Kansas.* Lawrence: University Press of Kansas, 1993.

AfriGeneas Forum. "Re: Langston Hughes's Ancestry." <http://afrigeneas.com/forum/index.cgi?noframes;read=18905>. Last visit 9/5/2004. Last update: 1/18/2002.

Allen, Robert Willis. "John Brown's Men at Arms, His Secret Backers, and His Opponents." <http://johnbrownsbody.net/Raiders.htm>. Webmaster: <mandelbroat@johnbrownsbody.net>. Last visit: 8/8/2002. Last update: 2000.

Ambler, Cathy. *Oak Hill Cemetery and the Rural Cemetery Movement.* 1990. Unpublished manuscript available at the Lawrence Public Library:

———. *Historic Cemeteries Tour of Lawrence.* Lawrence: Lawrence Convention & Visitors Bureau, undated. Self-guided tour pamphlet.

Andreas, A.T. *History of the State of Kansas.* V.1. Chicago: A.T. Andreas, 1883.

Armitage, Katie, lecturer. "Langston Hughes in Lawrence." *Biography of a City: Lawrence.* Session 7B Bart Koski (director). [Video recording] Videocassette (vhs) (25 min): Sound, color, and ½ inch tape, with B & W sequences. Academic Outreach Program, Division of Continuing Education, University of Kansas, 1998.

"The Conspirators Biographies." *John Brown and the Valley of the Shadows.* <http://iath.virginia.edu /jbrown/men.html>. Last visit: 8/29/2004. Last update: 3/21/95.

Baker, Jim. "Historical Significance: Pastors to Focus on Importance of Black Churches." *Lawrence Journal-World.* 17 July 2004.

Baumann, Roland M. "Introduction: A History of Recording Black Students at Oberlin College and the Story of the Missing Record." *RG 5/4/3 - Minority Student Records.* Oberlin College Archives. <http://www.oberlin.edu/archive/holdings/finding/RG5/SG4/S3/2002intro.html>. Last visit: 8/11/2004. Last update: 6/9/2004.

Bernard, Emily, ed. *Remember Me to Harlem: The Letters of Langston Hughes and Carl Van Vechten, 1925–1964.* New York: Alfred A. Knopf, 2002.

Berry, Faith. *Langston Hughes Before and Beyond Harlem.* Westport: Lawrence Hill, 1983.

Blockson, Charles L. *The Underground Railroad: First Person Narratives of Escape to Freedom in the North.* New York: Prentice Hall, 1987.

Butler, Maria. "Langston Hughes: Later Years." and "Church." <http://www.ci.lawrence.ks.us /langston_exhibit/church.html > Last visit: 8/14/2004.

Caldwell, E.F. *A Souvenir History of Lawrence, Kansas, 1898.* Lawrence: E.F. Caldwell, 1898.

"Charles Waddell Chestnutt." *Black History Facts.* <http://alfredoftexas.tripod.com /blackhistoryfacts/id8.html>. Last Visit: 8/11/2004.

Cheek, William F. and Aimee Lee Cheek. *John Mercer Langston and the Fight for Black Freedom, 1829 - 65.* Urbana: University of Illinois Press, 1989.

Cox, Thomas. *Blacks in Topeka, Kansas 1865–1915: A Social History.* Baton Rouge: Louisiana State University Press, 1982.

Dary, David and Steve Jansen, eds. *Pictorial History of Lawrence, Douglas County, Kansas.* Lawrence: Allen Books, 1992.

Daniels, Goldie Piper. *Rural Schools and Schoolhouses of Douglas County, Kansas.* Self-published. Lawrence: 1982.

Dickinson, Donald C. "A Bio-bibliography of Langston Hughes, 1902-1967." *The Langston Hughes Review: Official Publication of the Langston Hughes Society* 1.1 (1987): 44-6.

Douglas County, Kansas Marriages 1854–1884. VI. Lawrence: Douglas County, Kansas Genealogical Society, 1989.

Fagan, Mark. "Lawrence Shifting Focus to Mass Transit." *Lawrence Milestones: A Special Section Celebrating Lawrence's Sesquicentennial. Lawrence Journal World* 26 Sept. 2004: 18.

Fishel, Leslie H. and Benjamin Quarles. *The Black American: A Documentary History.* New York: William Morrow, 1970.

Francisco, Marci Ann. Personal interview by Denise Low. Lawrence, 7 Oct. 2004.

Haskins, James S. *The Life of Langston Hughes: Always Movin' On.* Trenton: Africa World Press, 1993.

Henrico County Order Book 1678-93, Levy Court 12 Oct1691, p. 249. Reprinted online at "Free African Americans of Virginia, North Carolina, South Carolina, Maryland, and Delaware: The history of the free African American community as told through the family history of most African Americans who were free in the Southeast during the colonial period." Compiled by Paul Heinegg. <http://www.freeafricanamericans.com/free_Indians.htm.> Last visit 17 Oct. 2004.

Hughes, Langston. *The Big Sea: Autobiography by Langston Hughes.* 1940. Rpt. New York: Hill Wang, 1994.

———. *The Langston Hughes Reader.* New York: George Braziller, 1958.

———. *Not Without Laughter.* 1930. Rpt. New York: Simon & Schuster, 1995.

———. *I Wonder as I Wander: An Autobiographical Journey.* 1956. New York: Hill and Wang 1993.

Hurst, Ian. Personal interview by Denise Low. Lawrence, 6 Oct. 2004.

Kelly, Jim, Narrator. Sunflower Journeys. *Cultural Diversity.* Program 1108. [Video recording] Videocassette (vhs) (29 min): Sound, color, and ½ inch tape, with B & W sequences. Dave Kendall and Claire Waring (producers). Topeka: Friends of KTWU/Channel 11, 1998.

Kendall, Dave and Claire Waring, producers. *1998 Viewers Guide, KTWU Channel 11,* Sunflower Journeys, Program #1108-Cultural Diversity; Langston Hughes. Topeka: Friends of KTWU, 1998.

Knight, Donald. Personal interview by T.F. Pecore Weso. Lawrence, 9 Sept. 2004.

Kohl, Robert, writer. "F. W. Barteldes." *Prominent Citizens of Lawrence in 1898.* <http://www.ci .lawrence.ks.us/local_histoty/citizens/barteld.htm>. Webmaster <lpl@cilawrence.ks.us>. Lawrence Public Library. Last visit: 8/10/2004. Last update: 1997.

Langston, John Mercer. *From the Virginia Plantations to the National Capitol.* Hartford: American Publishing Co., 1894.

Lawrence City Planning Commission. *A City Plan for Lawrence, Kansas: A Report Revised 1945–1948.* Kansas City: Hare & Hare City Planner, 1948.

"Lawrence Historic Resources Commission. Lawrence Historic Resources." Commission Agenda, 20 May 2004. City Commission. http://lawrenceplanning.org/documents /hrcagenda052004.pdf >. Last visit 8/11/2004.

Li, Kan, Site Designer. *Langston Hughes Committee, School Segment.* Lawrence High School Library, USD 497, Lawrence, KS. <http://library/lhs/usd497.org/LangstonHughesLawrence .html>. Webmaster: LHS Library. Last visit: 8/12/2004. Last update: 8/26/2002.

Libby, Jean, Hannah Geffert and Jimica Akinloye Kenyatta. "Hiram Revales Related to Men in John Brown's Army." <http://www.alliesforfreedom.org/allies.htm.> Last update 21 Dec. 1999. Last visit 9 Oct. 2004.

Marshall, Gary. Personal interview by Denise Low and T.F. Pecore Weso. Lawrence, 4 Sept. 2004.

Mathis, Joel. "History May Be Church's Salvation." *Lawrence Journal World.* 18 Oct. 2004:1.

Meltzer, Milton. *Langston Hughes: A Biography.* New York: Thomas Y. Crowell, 1968.

Moore, Heather. *Biographical Directory of the United States, 1774–present.* "John Mercer Langston, 1829-1897." Biographical Directory of the United States Congress. <http://bioguide.con-gress.gov/scripts/biodisplay.pl?index=L000074>. Last visit: 8/11/2004

Muller, Edward J. "Langston Hughes Remembered: A Documentary and a Commentary." *The Langston Hughes Review: Official Publication of the Langston Hughes Society* 3.2 (1984): 10-16.

New York Site Council. "New York Elementary History." *New York Elementary.* <http: //schools.usd497.org/newyork/History/History.htm>. Last visit: 8/10/2004. Last update: 6/7/2002.

Nichols, Charles H., ed. *Arna Bontemps and Langston Hughes: Letters 1925–1967.* New York: Dobbs Mead & Company, 1980.

Oberlin College Archives. *Oberlin Through History.* "John Mercer Langston (1829-1897)." Electronic Oberlin Group. <http://www.oberlin.edu/external/EOG/Default.html.>. <http:

//www.oberlin.edu/external/EOG/OYTT-images /JMLangston.htm.l>. Webmaster Gary Kornblith. Last visit: 8/11/2004. Last update: 8/6/2004.

O'Neal John, narrator. "Langston Hughes." *The Black Americans of Achievement Video Collection II*. [Video recording] Videocassette (vhs) (30 min): Sound, color, and ½ inch tape, with B & W sequences. Fabian-Baber, Inc., Communication Production. Schlessinger Video Productions, Division of Library Video Company: Bala Cynwyd, Pennsylvania., 1994.

Painter, Nell Irvin. *Exodusters: Black Migration to Kansas After Reconstruction*. New York: W. W. Norton, 1986.

Patterson, Louise. "Louise Patterson on Langston Hughes." *The Langston Hughes Review: Official Publication of the Langston Hughes Society*. 15.2 *(18 Oct. 1985): 39–51.*

Lawrence: Today and Yesterday. Supplement to the *Lawrence Daily Journal World*, 1913.

"Pinckney School History." <http://schools.usd497.org/pinckney/ PINCKNEY %20HIST.html>. Last visit: 9/10/2004.

Quarles, Benjamin. *Allies For Freedom: Blacks and John Brown*. New York: Oxford University Press, 1974.

Rampersad, Arnold. "Arnold Rampersad on Langston Hughes." *The Langston Hughes Review: Official Publication of the Langston Hughes Society* 15.2 (1997): 4-30.

———. *The Life of Langston Hughes 1902–1941: I, Too, Sing America*. Vol. 1. New York: Oxford University Press, 1986.

———. *The Life of Langston Hughes: 1941–1967 I Dream a World*. Vol.2. New York: Oxford University Press, 2002.

Rombeck, Terry. "Civil War Ancestor Unites Distant Cousins." *Lawrence Journal-World*. 29 August 2004: B1+.

Rountree, Helen. Pocahontas's People: *The Powhatan Indians of Virginia through Four Centuries*. Norman: University of Oklahoma Press, 1990.

Rowe, Elfriede Fischer. *Wonderful Old Lawrence*. Lawrence: The World Company, 1975.

———. *More About Wonderful Old Lawrence*. Lawrence: House of Usher, 1981.

"St. Luke AME Historic Landmark." 21 August 2001. Associated Press. http://www .ljworld.com/section/quantrill/story/63467 Last visit 9/6/2004.

Schultz, Beth, lecturer. "Growing up Black in Lawrence." *Biography of a City: Lawrence*. Session 7A: Bart Koski (director). [Video recording] Videocassette (vhs) (25 min): Sound, color, and ½ inch tape, with B & W sequences. Academic Outreach Program Division of Continuing Education, University of Kansas: The Programs, 1998.

Scott, Mark. "Langston Hughes of Kansas." *Kansas History* (1980): 3-28. Kansas State Historical Society. Rpt. <http://www.kshs.org/publicat/history/1980spring _scott.htm>. Last visit: 8/8/2004.

Sheridan, B. Richard. "Charles Henry Langston and the African American Struggle in Kansas." *Kansas History 22* (Winter 1999): 268-83. <http://www.kshs.org/publicat/history/1999wintersheridan.htm>. Pages 1 to 8. Last visit: 8/8/2004.

———. "From Slavery in Missouri to Freedom in Kansas: The Influx of Black Fugitives and Contrabands into Kansas, 1854-1865." *Kansas and the West: New Perspectives*. Ed. Rita Napier. Lawrence: University Press of Kansas, 2003.

Sutton, Paulette D. *Langston Hughes in Lawrence*. Prospectus for History 96: William M. Tuttle, Jr. Unpublished Manuscript, 1972.

Taylor, John, quoted in "Hughes: The Poet with a Ready Smile" by Anita Knopp. *Lawrence Journal World* 12 Nov.1974.

Thomas, Robert K. "A report on research of Lumbee origins." Unpublished manuscript, 1976. Quoted by Glenn Ellen Starr Stillings, "An Annotated Bibliography Supplement." http://linux.library.appstate.edu/Lumbee/16/THOM001.htm#Cherokee%20theory%20(Angus%20W.%20McLean) Last visit. 16 Oct. 2004. Last update 25 Apr 2002.

Tucker, E. S. *The Lawrence Memorial Album*. Lawrence: E. S. Tucker and Geo. O. Foster, 1895.

"Union Pacific Building." *Historic Preservation*. http://www.visitlawrence.com/media /storyideas/historicpreservation/. Last visit; 8/17/2004.

Walker, Alice. Public lecture. Langston Hughes Symposium. Lied Center, University of Kansas, Lawrence. 31 Jan. 2002.

Waugaman, Sandra and Danielle Moretti-Langholtz. *We're Still Here: Contemporary Virginia Indians Tell Their Story*. Richmond: Palari Publishing, 2000.

Wiley, George. "Center Profile: Ninth Street Missionary Baptist Church." The Pluralism Project. Last visit: 8/7/2004. Last update: 6/3/2004. <http://www.pluralism.org/research /profiles/ display.php?profile=72401 >.

Williams, W. William. *History of Astabula County, Ohio*. Philadelphia: Williams Brothers: 1878. 23-45. <http://solomonspalding.com/SRP/saga2/1878Ast2.htm>

Appendix 1
City Directories of Lawrence:
Selected Listings for Langston Hughes and
Related References

City directories for Lawrence range from the 1860s to the 1920s; and from 1961 to the present. These are available at the Lawrence Public Library, in the genealogy section; the University of Kansas libraries; Kansas Historical Society; and other institutions. Different private companies published the books, so format and information change from year to year. Beginning with the 1902-03 edition, street listings are included intermittently as well as individual and business listings.

Abbreviations are reproduced as they appear in the directory. The reference to ethnic origin is quoted as it appears, "c" or "col'd" for "Colored," for example. "R" refers to the resident who owns the house, while "b" refers to a boarder or renter. In some years, the occupations are listed; others they are not. If a man is a head of a household, the wife and other adult women may or may not be listed afterwards in parentheses. Minor children are never listed. In 1915, for example, Homer Clark is the resident of 732 Alabama St., and no other residents are listed with him. Nonetheless, his son Gwyn "Kit" Clark lived with him, his wife Carrie Langston Clark; her son Langston Hughes; and also Mary Langston.

The earlier entries describe the general location a person lives, in relationship to the block or corner. The numbered streets had proper names during this time span, such as Henry, Winthrop, Pinckney, and Warren. They were named for Revolutionary War heroes.

The directory shows some surprises, such as C.S. [sic] Langston, Langston Hughes's grandfather, and presumably all his household living at 732 Alabama St. in 1886, not 1888 as reported in some sources. He is listed as a farmer, not a grocer. And his son D.W. (Desalines) is living in the house next to him, at 726 Alabama, with a business listing as a barber. Charles Langston's Douglas County farmland is listed in the 1890-91 and 1893 directories, after he moved to town. The directory shows that Charles Langston is a business associate in the Burns and Co. grocery business in 1890-91; but in 1893, after Charles's death, N.T. (Nathaniel) is listed as a participant. In 1907 Langston Hughes's father, James Nathaniel Hughes, is living in the 732 Alabama St. house, and he is a "stenogr.," a stenographer. No biographies make mention of his presence in Lawrence.

In 1923, Mary Reed, a foster parent to Langston Hughes after his grandmother died, is listed as a widow at 731 New York St. In the 1925-26 directory, Walter Campbell is the resident at that address. He married Mary Reed, according to biographer Arnold Rampersad (V.1 234). In a newspaper report of Hughes's 1942 visit to St. Luke A.M.E. church in Lawrence, "Mrs. Walter Campbell of this city" is described as his "aunt."

Abbreviations:

a	acres	Ma	Massachusetts St.
b	boarder	nr	near
bet	between	po	post office
c	"colored"	r	residence
col'd.	"colored"	sec	section
es	east side	wid	widow
lab	laborer	ws	west side

1883

Langston, D.W. (col'd), r. es New Jersey bet. Henry & Warren

Langston, Mrs. D.E., (col'd), r. New Jersey bet. Henry & Warren

1886

Langston, C.S. (col'd) farmer r. 732 Alabama

Langston, D.W., (col'd) barber r. 726 Alabama

from the Business Directory:

Langston, D.W., Henry, west of Massachusetts

1890–91

Langston, CH (Burns + Co) r 732 Alabama

from the Business Directory:

Burns + Co (Richard B + CH Langston) groceries 820 Mass.

from Douglas County listings:

Langston, C.H. sec 16 Wakarusa 122 a[cres] po Lawrence

1893

Langston, N.T., Burns & Co. groc. r. 732 Alabama

Langston, Mrs. M., col, r. 732 Alabama

from the Business Directory:

Burns + Co (RB and NT Langston) grocers

from Douglas County listings:

Langston, C.H., sec. 16 Wakarusa, 26 a[cres] p o Lawrence

1896

Langston, Carrie M. col. Dep. Clk Dist. Court r. 732 Alabama

Langston, Mary S. col. r. 732 Alabama

Fuller, A.N. r. end Henry [St.]

1898

Langston, Carrie M. 732 Alabama

Langston, Mary S. 732 Alabama

1900–01

Langston, Mary (c) r. 732 Alabama

Langston, Nellie (c), r. 903 Tennessee [widow of Nat. Langston]

1902–03

Langston, Mamie (c) res 824 New Jersey

Langston, Mary S. (c) res 732 Alabama

Hughes, Carrie M. (c) res 732 Alabama

1905

Reed, Ja W, lab, r 731 New York

Fuller, Arthur N, r bet Winthrop and Warren nr city limit

1907

Langston, Mrs. Mary S. (c) r 732 Alabama

Hughes, James N. (c) stenogr r 732 Alabama

Porter, J.A. (c) plasterer, r 736 Alabama [first residence listed at this address]

Reed, James W (c) lab 731 New York

1908–09

Langston, Mary S. (c) b 731 New York

Reed, James W (c), sewer man Kennedy Plumbing Co. r. 731 New York

Street Listings:

Alabama St.: 726 Lewis Overstreet (c), Robert Thomas (c);

  732 Bratton, Othel F. (Frances M) eng. Vit B & T Co.

New York St.: 723 F.T. Evans 731 J.W. Reed [No residence is listed between 723 and 731 New
  York from this directory to the 1930s, when this series of directories ends. The Reeds apparently had livestock and a garden in the open space. Deeds to these lots do not record
  transactions before the 1940s. A barn at the back of 727 N.Y. St. must have been used by
  the Reeds.]

1911

Langston, Mary S (wid Charles H), r 732 Alabama

Street Listings:

Alabama St.: 726 H. U. Monroe (c); 732 Mrs. M. S. Langston

New York St.:   731 J. W. Reed

1913–1914

Langston, Mary (c) (wid Charles H), b 731 New York

Reed, Wilson (c) (Mary J) lab r 731 New York

from Street and other Listings:

Alabama St.: 724 Frank Matthews; 726 [no entry]; 732 Lewis Renfrown (c)

Hotels: Eldridge 701-9 Massachusetts; Fairfax 708-10 Massachusetts; Santa Fe 700 Connecticut; Lawrence House 811 Vermont; Place House 846 New Hampshire; Savoy Hotel
  846 Vermont.

Seeds-Retail: Barteldes Seed Co 804 Massachusetts; Busch W J 608 Massachusetts.

Theatres: Airdome 834 New Hampshire; Aurora 733 Massachusetts; Bowersock 648 Massachusetts; Grand 736 Massachusetts; Nickle 708 Massachusetts; Oread 907 Massachusetts;
  Palace 633 Massachusetts

Churches include: St. Luke Pastor J.F.C. Taylor, 260 members; Warren St. rev. G.N. Jackson

1915

Langston, Mary (c) (wid Charles), b 732 Alabama

Clark, Homer (c) (Carrie) lab r 732 Alabama

Reed, Wilson (c) (Mary J) lab Kennedy Plumbing Co, r 731 New Jersey

Reed, James W (c) (Mary J) lab r 731 New York

from Street Listings:

Alabama St.: 726 Mrs. S.E. Johnson (c) resident (widow Richard); 732 Homer Clark (c)

New York St.: 731 J.W. Reed

1917

from Street Listings:

Alabama St.: 726 Mrs. S.E. Johnson (c); 732 J.C. Bryant

New York St.: 731 JW Reed

1919

Hughes, Joseph E (c) (Lethna B) presser Lawrence Pantorium r 732 Alabama

Reed, James W (c) (Mary) lab 731 NY

from Street Listings:

Alabama St.: 726 Mrs. Susan E.P. Johnson (c); 732 J.E. Hughes (c)

1923

Hughes, Joseph (Lethna) Janitor Jr High Sch r 732 Ala.

from Street Listings:

Alabama St.: 726 Anna Jackson; 732 Joseph Hughes

New York St.: 731 Mary J. Reed, widow

1925–26

Hughes, Joseph (Lethna) cook Rock Chalk Café h 732 Ala.

from Street Listings:

Alabama St.: 726 Mrs. Angeline Suttles; 732 Joseph Hughes

New York St.: 731 Walter Campbell

Appendix 2
Mortgage and Deed Sources

A mortgage and two bills of sale verify the Langston family's ownership of two-and-a-half lots (south side of lot 7, lot 8, and lot 9 of block 12) of Lane Place subdivision (Alabama St.). However, the Douglas County registry of deeds shows no Langston deeds, even though they had legal title during the registry's historic range.

Deeds to these properties all begin with James S. Emery, who was a developer who specialized in contacting U.S. veterans of the War of 1812, or their widows, and offering to purchase their "Military Land Warrant' titles, or land granted as payment for military service. They lived in the eastern states and presumably preferred quick cash to ownership of distant Kansas lands. He acquired large holdings of Lawrence property in the 1870s and 1880s. S.A. Northway, named on the Alabama St. deeds, was most likely the Ohio veteran who was a state representative and attorney (Williams 23-45).

In 1895, "Sarah J. Langston" was the beneficiary of any surplus money in case of foreclosure on the 726 Alabama St. property. Her identity is unknown.

John Warren Clark was an African American attorney who performed legal services for many Lawrence African Americans. He is pictured in *A Souvenir History of Lawrence, Kansas, 1898,* as a member of the Douglas County bar (Caldwell 62).

A.N. Fuller could be the "mortgage man" Langston Hughes wrote about in his autobiography. He appears in the city directories as A.N. Fuller in 1893-94 and 1896 and as Arthur N. Fuller, 1905. In the 1893-94 directory, he is listed as a "dealer in minerals."

The taxman must have been as much of a threat to the Langstons as the mortgage man. Both bills of sale mention taxes.

The Register of Deeds office in Douglas County, Kansas, has the following records relating to the Langston family:

Mortgage of property, 726 Alabama St., 28 Feb. 1895 (south half, lot 7)
"Indenture" between Mary S. Langston and A.N. Fuller of Lawrence National Bank: $125.00 loan made against the south half of lot no. 7, block 12, Lane Place subdivision in Lawrence, Kansas. Two promissory notes were due March 1, 1896 ($25.00) and March 1, 1897 ($100.00), at 8% per annum, payable annually. In case of default and foreclosure and sale, any amount remaining after expenses would go to Sarah S. Langston.

Notary Public was Alfred Whitman and Register of Deeds was James Brooks.

Registry of Deeds, 726 Alabama St. (south half, lot 7)
The land record originates with S.A. Northway's wife granting J.S. Emery deed to the land in 1887, but this was not filed until 1920. The next deed filed on this property was by E. C.

Freeman's wife, granting it to Angeline Suttles, 23 July 1925, for the south half of lot 7, block 12, Lane Place subdivision of Lawrence.

The record omits the years between 1887 and 1920, when the Langstons owned the property.

Bill of sale, 726 Alabama St., 6 November 1909 (north half, lot 8)

"Indenture" of Mary S. Langston, widow, and Carrie M., Hughes, formerly Langston, of Douglas Co., selling property to Eli C. Freeman of Manhattan County [sic], Kansas for $175.00, for the north half of lot 8, block 12, Lane Place subdivision in Lawrence, Kansas, subject to taxes of the year 1909.

Notary Public was John M. Newlin and Register of Deeds was Floyd L. Lawrence.

Registry of Deeds, 726 Alabama St. (north half, lot 8)

The first deed filed was by E.C. Freeman's wife, granting title to Angeline Suttles, 23 July 1925, for the north half of lot 8, block 12, Lane Place subdivision of Lawrence.

Bill of sale, 732 Alabama St., 13 Oct. 1915 Deed Record No. 93 (south half, lot 8 and lot 9)

"Indenture" of Carrie M. Hughes Clark and Homer S. Clark in Douglas County, Lawrence, selling property to John L. Kilworth of Douglas County, Kansas, for: "one dollar and other valuable considerations," for the south half of lot 8 and all of lot 9, block 12, Lane Place subdivision in Lawrence. The words "50 Cent Rev. Stamp" are drawn on the deed, but the actual stamp is missing.

Notary Public was J. Hilky and Register of Deeds was Floyd L. Lawrence. The document was executed by the deputy Register of Deeds, George Wetzel.

Registry of Deeds, 732 Alabama St. (south half, lot 8)

The land record originates with S.A. Northway's wife granting J.S. Emery deed to the land in 1887, but this is not filed until 1920. The next deed was filed by John L. Kilworth's wife to John W. Clark, 2 June 1916, filed 23 May 1922; and from John W. Clark's wife to Joseph E. Hughes, 4 Feb. 1928, filed 7 Feb. 1928. Again, no record remains of the years the Langstons had legal title to the property.

Registry of Deeds, 730–32 Alabama St. (lot 9)

The first deed filed is by S.A. Northway's wife to J.S. Emery, 7 March 1887 and filed 3 June 1920. John L. Kilworth's wife deeded the land to John W. Clark, dated 20 June 1917, but it was not filed until 1922. John W. Clark's wife deeded the land to Joseph E. Hughes in Feb. 1928.

Appendix 3
Langston Hughes in Kansas 1932 to 1965

A listing of Langston Hughes's adult trips and connections to Kansas includes, but is not limited to, the following:

1932
Hughes appeared at the University of Kansas for a poetry reading, sponsored by an African American sorority, Alpha Kappa Alpha. He stayed with Mary Reed Campbell and attended church with her at St. Luke A.M.E. His mother Carrie Clark also visited Lawrence at that time (Rampersad v.1 234).

1937
Hughes contributed the poem "Let America Be America Again" to *Anthology of Kansas Verse, Kansas Magazine,* selected by Kenneth Porter of Southwest College. It was reprinted from *Esquire.*

5 April 1939
Hughes read poems in Kansas City, 8 pm, at the Little Theater of Municipal Auditorium, sponsored by Worker's Institute of Greater Kansas City, to a "predominately white audience." Introduction was by Thomas A. Webster of the Kansas City Urban League. He said "abolition of color prejudice could create in America a true democracy." (*Kansas City Star*).

The newspaper also reported the poet "visited Lawrence this morning, calling on old friends and relatives."

Summer 1939
The *Kansas City Star* (10 Feb. 1940) reported, from an unidentified source, Hughes was writing in Carmel, California, and had visited Kansas City "last summer."

25–6 Nov. 1942
Hughes read poetry at the Kansas Vocational School auditorium in Topeka, Kansas (*Topeka Capitol*) and the next day, as reported by the Lawrence paper, at St. Luke A.M.E. Church. He was assisted by Nadine Bower of the KU fine arts dept. and by a choir. The paper reports, "Mrs. Walter Campbell of this city is his aunt." Mary Reed had married Walter Campbell after James W. Reed died. Hughes also appeared in Kansas City during this visit.

1957
University of Kansas acquisitions librarian Donald Dickinson contacted Langston Hughes regarding copies of his publications. Dickinson and library director Robert Vosper wanted to initiate a collection of his published works. Hughes donated several publications. This began the Langston Hughes Collection now housed at the Spencer Research Library.

1958

Hughes appeared at the University of Kansas Student Union Oct. 7, to read poetry, with jazz band accompaniment. The audience was estimated at 900 students. The Spencer Special Collections online exhibit describes the event: "His arrival was enthusiastically awaited and he had a full schedule while here. In addition to a public presentation, he rehearsed with a jazz quartet that would accompany him in his program, met with several classes, attended a presentation by the *A Capella* choir, lunched with friends and officials, and attended a book signing and reception at the Union."

25 April 1965

Hughes appeared at the University of Kansas, Student Union, for a poetry reading and lecture, "Life Makes Poetry." The Spencer Research Library has a record of this lecture.

Also Available from Mammoth Publications:

Caryn Mirriam-Goldberg, *Reading the Body: Poems* (2004), $5.00

Denise Low, *New and Selected Poems 1980–1999* (2000),
originally published by Penthe Press, $12.95

Denise Low, *Touching the Sky: Essays* (1994),
originally published by Penthe Press, $15.00

E. Donald Two-Rivers, *Powwows, Fat Cats, and Other Indian Tales,* $12.00

Send cost plus $2.50 shipping and handling to Mammoth Publications, 1916
Stratford Rd., Lawrence, KS 66044. Kansas residents, please add 7% sales tax.

Direct queries to mammothpubs@hotmail.com

Denise Low, Ph.D., is chair of the English Dept. at Haskell Indian Nations Univ. and visiting professor, Univ. of Richmond. She co-edited *New Perspectives on Leslie Marmon Silko's Ceremony*, a special issue of *American Indian Culture and Research Journal* (UCLA 2004). Her articles and reviews appear in *Studies in American Indian Literature, American Indian Quarterly*, and *Midwest Quarterly*. Other publications include ten books of poetry and personal essays.

T. F. Pecore Weso, M.A., teaches U.S. history at Longview Community College in Lee's Summit, Mo. He has authored articles published in *Mid-America Folklore Journal, American Indian Culture and Research Journal, Confluence of Cultures*, and others. He has given presentations to the Southwest/ Texas Popular Culture Association, the Kansas Folklore Society, Imagination & Place, and Avila College. He is a member of the Menominee Indian Nation of Wisconsin.